MASTERING MULTIFAMILY
REAL ESTATE SALES

EXECUTIVE EDITION

Written by

L.S. Shepherd

LSS Publishing & Media

Executive Edition

Printed in the United States of America

First Edition

Publisher:

LSS Publishing & Media

MasteringMultifamilyRE.com

ISBN (Executive Edition): 979-8-9950215-0-6

For permissions and inquiries:
LShepherd@LSSPublishingandmedia.com

ACKNOWLEDGMENTS

To my family — your unwavering patience, support and belief gave me the strength to write with purpose and conviction. You are the heart behind the vision.

PREFACE

Before every great work, there is a moment of stillness — a quiet space between belief and becoming. Mastering Multifamily Real Estate Sales was born in that stillness. I didn't set out to write another guide. It was meant to be a catalyst — a mentor in book form, a source of wisdom and guidance for those called to build something greater than themselves.

It stands as both a guide and a testimony — proof that when purpose is fueled by courage, results exceed imagination.

This is more than business; it's ministry through excellence.

❖

To every reader who has chosen to grow through these pages — may your journey be met with clarity, courage, and renewed confidence to reach higher and create meaningful impact.

May the lessons ahead expand your perspective, equip you with sound knowledge, and strengthen the wisdom needed to thrive in both business and life.

Let every insight you gain become a seed for growth — cultivating prosperity, legacy, and fulfillment that endures.

INTRODUCTION

Real estate is more than contracts and closings — it's communication, knowledge, and consistency.

Mastering Multifamily Real Estate Sales was created for both new and seasoned agents who are ready to evolve — to expand from residential transactions into the multifamily arena with confidence, clarity, and a strategic understanding of what it takes to succeed at scale.

This book is structured to serve as both a classroom and a compass. It walks you through every stage of multifamily sales — mindset, market knowledge, deal analysis, wealth strategies, and legacy-building — with practical exercises and reflection prompts designed to convert knowledge into mastery.

As you turn each page, you'll notice two parallel themes:

Professional Mastery — skill-building, analysis, systems, and growth.

Personal Empowerment — faith, mindset, and leadership.

I wrote this guide as someone who has stood where you stand: eager to grow, sometimes uncertain, but always determined. Every chapter is a conversation — not from expert to student, but from one professional to another who understands that success takes both strategy and spirit.

Remember this truth: mastery is not a title — it's a process of becoming.

And you are becoming everything you were created to be.

Welcome to your next level.

— LS. Shepherd

TABLE OF CONTENTS

PART I — FOUNDATIONS & MINDSET

PART II — PROFESSIONAL PRACTICE

PART III — ADVANCED SKILLS & ANALYTICAL MASTERY

PART IV — WEALTH, LEGACY & LEADERSHIP

PART V — LEGACY, LEADERSHIP & LONG-TERM INFLUENCE

PART I

FOUNDATIONS & MINDSET

Every successful multifamily professional begins in the same place — not with numbers, contracts, or listings, but with clarity of purpose and identity.

Part I is designed to ground you in who you are becoming as an agent and advisor.

Before you can confidently analyze deals, guide investors, or navigate complex transactions, you must first understand your "*why*," develop an investor's mindset, and align your work with intention rather than urgency.

These chapters establish the internal framework that supports everything that follows.

Here, you will explore the mindset shifts that separate transactional agents from trusted professionals. You will learn how purpose drives consistency, how perspective shapes opportunity, and why confidence is built long before the first deal is closed. This part is not about speed or tactics — it is about foundation.

Consider Part I your orientation into the discipline of multifamily real estate. What you build here will quietly influence every decision, conversation, and strategy you apply throughout the rest of this book — and throughout your career.

Chapter 1 — The Purpose-Driven Agent

Every successful agent has a story

Some begin with necessity, others with curiosity, but all share a moment when a decision was made:

"I'm building something that lasts."

The multifamily space demands clarity of intention.

It isn't only about units and rent rolls; it's about people, communities, and stability.

As a real estate advisor, your greatest asset isn't your license — it's your perspective.

The professionals who build enduring success are those who define their why early and return to it often. That clarity becomes an internal compass when a deal falls through, a client disappears, or the market shifts overnight.

Seeing Every Property as a Living Economy

Each transaction you touch sets off a chain reaction: jobs, families, contractors, lenders, inspectors, and city departments all move because of that single deal.

When you begin to view each property as a micro-community instead of a commission, everything changes — your presence, your priorities, your purpose.

> FIELD INSIGHT — Angela's First Multifamily Deal
>
> When Angela, a newly licensed multifamily agent, sold her first twelve unit building, she didn't just close a deal. She created affordable homes for twelve families, stabilized a neglected block, and helped a retired owner reinvest his equity into a passive-income property.
>
> What could have been a single transaction became a multi-layered win for everyone involved — proof that one thoughtful deal can ripple far beyond the closing table.
>
> ***— Excerpt from the author's field notes***

Define Your Mission

Write a two-sentence mission statement that captures why you sell real estate. Keep it visible — on your desk, mirror, or phone lock screen — and revisit it at the start of each quarter.

"I connect investors to properties that build stronger communities and generational wealth."

Let your mission guide every marketing piece, client conversation, and negotiation you enter.

As you reflect, consider:

- What impact do I want my work to have on my community?
- How do my daily actions reflect my larger vision?
- Which types of clients energize me — and which drain me?
- Where have I allowed money or fear to blur my sense of direction?

Real estate is unpredictable. Markets shift, clients hesitate, deals fall apart — and fear whispers that you're not ready.

But the agent advisors who thrive are those who move from mission, not fear.

When your motivation is rooted in service, clarity, and stability, uncertainty loses its power.

Your confidence becomes contagious; clients feel it before you speak a word.

Allow Your Mission to Evolve

Your mission isn't static — it grows as you do

At first, it may center on financial security; later, it may mature into legacy, mentorship, or community transformation.

Every milestone and challenge is a chance to refine it.

The clearer your "Why", the quicker you'll recover when the market tests you.

Your vision drives your goals. Your goals shape your systems. Your systems protect your energy and sustain your career.

An agent anchored in vision never asks, *"Do I belong here?"*

The answer is already yes — because conviction is the proof.

What's Next

You've laid the foundation of who you are and why you serve. That clarity becomes your advantage in every deal you touch.

In the next chapter, we'll build on that foundation by translating intention into performance — developing the mindset and systems that turn confidence into consistency

Chapter 2 — Understanding Your Why

In real estate — especially multifamily — your Why is not a slogan or a marketing tagline.

It's the steady conviction behind every phone call, showing, and negotiation.

It's the quiet reason you keep going when motivation fades or deals fall apart.

Your "Why" shapes your habits.

It defines how you respond under pressure, how you show up for clients, and how you interpret success.

When your Why is clear, your energy is focused.
When it's not, you'll find yourself chasing trends, leads, and approval instead of building momentum.

Purpose vs. Motivation

Motivation can change daily — it's emotional fuel

Purpose, however, is directional; it keeps you moving through uncertainty.

You can't depend on inspiration to call clients, nurture relationships, or follow up after rejections.

But if you know your Why, you'll do the work even when the spark is gone.

Ask yourself:

"If I stopped selling today, what impact would I miss making?"

That answer usually points directly to your purpose.

Your "Why" Is a Filter, Not a Burden

Many real estate advisors believe they have to say yes to everything — every client, every opportunity, every idea.

But when you're rooted in purpose, you become more selective.

Your Why becomes a filter that keeps you from scattering your focus.

Not every client deserves your calendar, and not every opportunity matches your vision.

When you begin operating from that filter, you trade stress for strategy.

> FIELD INSIGHT — Marcus's Turning Point
>
> Marcus was an ambitious new advisor who said yes to everyone.
> He worked long hours, took every showing, and marketed properties he didn't even believe in.
>
> At first, it looked like hustle — but after six months, he was exhausted and questioning whether he'd chosen the right field.
>
> One evening, Marcus revisited his journal and realized his original reason for entering multifamily real estate was stability — both financial and emotional.
>
> He wanted to help families and investors find predictable wealth.
> The chaos he'd created by over-committing was the opposite of what he valued. So, he made a rule: if an opportunity didn't align with his Why, he'd politely decline it.
>
> Within three months, his income grew — not because he worked more, but because he worked intentionally.
>
> *— Excerpt from the author's field notes*

Clarity Creates Confidence

Confidence doesn't come from sales numbers or social media followers — it comes from consistency.

It grows when you know what you stand for and deliver it repeatedly.

When you understand your Why, your message to clients becomes magnetic.

Clarity eliminates competition because it creates identity.
You stop sounding like everyone else and start sounding like yourself.

“The clearer your "Why", the more aligned your clients will be.”

Practice Exercise — The Alignment Audit

Take out a notepad or open a blank document.

List your top five professional priorities for this quarter.

Next to each one, ask yourself:

- Does this priority serve my purpose or distract from it?
- Does it align with my vision or simply fill my schedule?
- Is it building momentum or draining energy?

If it doesn’t serve your purpose, either delegate it, defer it, or delete it. Staying anchored to your "Why" keeps you moving strategically, not reactively.

Legacy Over Limelight

The best agents don’t chase visibility — they build legacy.

Your Why is what people remember when the transaction is done. It’s what separates the advisor who closes a deal
from the advisor who transforms a neighborhood.

When your actions and systems reflect your deeper purpose, your reputation compounds.

Visibility may open doors — but legacy keeps them open for generations.

Purpose in Action

Your Why isn't a speech you give — it's a life you live.

It shows up in how you answer emails, handle setbacks, and celebrate others' wins.

It's present in the way you follow up with clients months after closing, just to ask:

"How's everything going?"

That consistency turns purpose into presence — and presence into prosperity.

What's Next

- Your "Why" defines your focus.
- Your focus shapes your brand.
- Your brand attracts the right clients.

The clearer your Why, the faster your success aligns with your peace.

In the next chapter, we'll take this clarity and apply it to performance — creating systems, routines, and daily habits that keep your vision in motion and your growth intentional.

Chapter 3 — Entering the Multifamily Industry: A Step-by-Step Blueprint for New and Transitioning Agents

Transitioning into multifamily real estate is like learning a new language.

The rhythm, vocabulary, and expectations differ from traditional residential sales.

While the fundamentals of service and integrity remain the same, the strategy, pace, and mindset demand an upgrade.

Many agents are told to avoid commercial deals — to "stick to residential" or "refer it out" because multifamily is a "beast," which can intimidate even experienced professionals.

That mindset alone is discouraging and limits opportunity.

Yes, multifamily is more complex — but the truth is this:

It's not a beast — it's a blueprint.
One that rewards preparation, patience, and knowledge.

Commercial real estate doesn't test your limits — it reveals your capacity to rise beyond them.

This chapter walks you through that transition — not theoretically, but practically — so you can begin your multifamily journey with structure and confidence.

Redefine Your Identity as an Advisor

Excellence begins with perception — how you define your role defines your results.

You are no longer just a *"home seller."*

You are a **multifamily strategist** — a consultant who advises on cash flow, tenant stability, and long-term portfolio growth.

"The words you use determine the doors you open."

Update your bios, website, and social media captions to reflect your new focus.

Instead of saying, "I help people find homes," say:

"I help investors and owners build scalable income through multifamily assets."

Clarity attracts opportunity.

Build Your Knowledge Foundation

Authority grows from mastery — and mastery begins with understanding how multifamily properties operate, perform, and appreciate over time.

You're no longer assessing curb appeal or bedroom count; you're evaluating revenue engines, operational systems, and economic patterns.

Your learning focus shifts from:

features → **performance**
aesthetics → **efficiency**
emotion → **economics**

Begin by grounding yourself in the systems, patterns, and mechanics that drive multifamily performance.

Behind every successful property is a predictable structure — one built on income flow, expense behavior, tenant demand, and strategic ownership decisions.

Commit to understanding the core drivers of multifamily success:

- Income Structure — how rents, fees, and ancillary income stabilize and grow
- Expense Behavior — how operating costs rise, fall, or stay fixed
- Operational Efficiency — how management quality increases or erodes NOI
- Market Dynamics — how population, employment, and development influence demand
- Value Creation — how renovations, repositioning, or better management elevate performance
- Deal Flow & Underwriting Logic — how investors evaluate, compare, and prioritize opportunities

The deeper your knowledge, the more naturally you transition from *"showing properties"* to **interpreting investments.**

As you refine this mindset, immerse yourself in environments that sharpen your judgment — market reports, investor conversations, property tours, and financial case studies. Each provides context, pattern recognition, and real-world nuance you cannot learn from theory alone.

Exposure builds instinct, and the more you engage with real properties, real numbers, and real investor discussions, the more naturally you begin to think, speak, and evaluate like an investor. You'll begin noticing trends others overlook — shifts in rental demand, patterns in operational inefficiency, and indicators of untapped value.

Clarity grows into confidence. When you understand the mechanics, the deals begin to "*speak,*" and you develop the analytical fluency your clients rely on.

Identify Your Ideal Client

Not every investor is your investor.... Clarity attracts opportunity.

Choosing the right client type isn't just about preference — it determines the pace of your business, the complexity of your deals, and the depth of expertise you must develop.

When you know exactly who you serve, your positioning sharpens, your marketing becomes more effective, and your conversations become more confident.

Decide whether you'll specialize in:

- Small owners (2–10 units) and first-time investors
- Mid-level owners (10–50 units) pursuing value-add strategies
- Institutional or syndication clients (50+ units) seeking scalability

Each group has different expectations:

• Small investors → affordability + guidance
They need education, clarity, and patient support. These clients value

advisors who simplify the process, explain terms, help them compare financing options, and guide them through their first cash-flow decision.

• **Mid-level operators → value-add + efficiency**

These investors focus on upside potential, renovation strategy, operational efficiency, and long-term scaling. They expect sharper analysis, clearer rent-growth projections, and advisors who speak the language of cost, return, and repositioning.

• **Institutional clients → scalability + data + execution**

These seasoned investors rely on data modeling, market analytics, deal velocity, and professional-grade communication. They value precision, speed, and advisors who understand the interplay of portfolio strategy and market timing.

Your ideal client shapes:

- The way you present deals
- The type of education you provide
- The relationships you build
- The lenders and partners you align with
- The marketing content you create
- The complexity of your deal analysis

When you try to serve "*everyone*," you dilute your message and exhaust your energy.

But when you commit to the group whose goals match your strengths, you build a brand that feels intentional, credible, and trustworthy.

Align your communication style, marketing, and analysis depth with the group you understand best.

Your ideal client is the client your skills naturally elevate.

Create a Market Intelligence System

Knowledge of your market is your leverage — not just for finding deals, but for earning credibility.

Investors rely on advisors who understand the numbers beneath the surface: pricing patterns, demand cycles, rent pressures, and the subtle movements happening long before a property ever hits the MLS.

A market intelligence system transforms you from a reactive agent into a proactive strategist.

It positions you as someone who can interpret the market rather than merely report it.

Set up a tracking sheet or CRM tag for:

- Active listings & recent sales — reveals supply, demand, and pricing pressure
- Average cap rates & price-per-unit — shows how investors value income locally
- Common renovation costs & rent ranges — informs value add potential instantly
- Key landlords, owners, and property managers — builds familiarity with local operators, patterns, and off-market opportunities

This tracking system becomes your personal database of trends, behaviors, and opportunities.

Within 30 days, patterns begin to appear — which submarkets are tightening, where rents are climbing, where cap rates are compressing, and which owners may be preparing to sell.

Within 90 days, you'll start predicting opportunities before they hit the MLS.

You'll recognize underpriced deals faster, see red flags sooner, and interpret value-add potential with greater clarity.

A strong market intelligence system does more than keep you informed **— it makes you the advisor investors trust before they trust anyone else.**

Cross-Reference: *See Chapter 6 — "Market Mastery: Leveraging Data to Predict Opportunity".*

Build Your Professional Network

Relationships are the true currency of real estate.

In multifamily, they're not optional — they are the infrastructure that supports your growth.

Every successful multifamily advisor stands on the strength of the professionals around them.

Your network determines:

- How quickly your deals move
- The quality of information you receive
- The confidence investors place in your guidance
- Your ability to solve problems before they escalate

In this space, you're not just building contacts — you're building a reputation ecosystem.

Your circle should include:

- Commercial lenders & credit-union officers — those who understand DSCR, risk tiers, and market lending appetite
- Property managers & maintenance vendors — the people who know what buildings really cost to operate
- Title and escrow officers with multifamily experience — essential for navigating complex ownership structures
- Inspectors and contractors familiar with building systems — especially HVAC, roofing, plumbing, and electrical, which directly impact NOI

Each relationship adds a layer of expertise you can bring back to your clients.

When an investor asks, *"What will it cost to upgrade the HVAC?"* or *"Can this building qualify for agency financing?"* — having the right professional on speed dial is the difference between guessing and advising.

Attend investor meetups monthly — not to pitch, but to listen.

Listening reveals:

- What investors are struggling with
- What opportunities they're chasing
- What financial strategies they're using
- What property types are gaining interest

You're not just collecting business cards; you're collecting insights.

Over time, these relationships compound into **reputation equity** — trust that grows before you enter the room and stays long after you leave it.

A strong network doesn't just support your business.

It anchors your credibility and elevates your value as a multifamily strategist.

Understand Financing Structures

Numbers tell the story; learn to read them fluently.

In multifamily real estate, financing isn't just the method investors use to acquire property — it is the financial framework that determines whether a deal is stable, scalable, or too risky to pursue.

Understanding financing structures elevates you from "*agent*" to **multifamily investment advisor.**

Why? Because the best deals aren't found — they're structured.

Most multifamily acquisitions rely on layered financing, each with different risk profiles, closing timelines, and performance expectations:

- **Conventional loans** underwritten primarily by NOI — ideal for stable, cash-flowing properties
- **Bridge loans** used for heavy value-add projects, reposition strategies, or properties needing significant operational improvement
- **Private capital or syndication models** blending equity with debt — often used for larger assets or group investments where scale is key

Each structure influences:

- The type of buyer the property attracts
- How quickly a deal can close
- The level of risk the investor must take
- The property's ability to weather market shifts
- The long-term viability of the investment

Regardless of the loan product, lenders evaluate one metric above all:

The property's ability to pay for itself.

That's where DSCR becomes essential.

DSCR = Net Operating Income ÷ Annual Debt Service

A DSCR of **1.20** means the property produces 20% more income than its mortgage requires — the safety cushion lenders look for across all financing types.

This single metric influences approval decisions, interest rates, loan terms, and ultimately, the long-term health of the property.

Whether the financing is conventional, bridge, or equity-based, DSCR is the metric lenders use to judge:

- Repayment strength
- Operational stability
- Risk level
- Cash-flow reliability
- Overall deal viability

When you understand financing structures, you stop selling properties and start engineering solutions.

You can guide your clients toward the loan products that best support their strategy, timeline, and risk tolerance. You can also identify when a "great deal" is actually a financing nightmare.

The formulas, calculations, and full application of **DSCR** — along with other lending metrics — will be taught in detail in **Chapter** 7, where you'll learn how to evaluate deals the way lenders and investors do.

FIELD INSIGHT — When Numbers Speak Louder Than Credit

When DeShawn, a first-time multifamily investor, applied for a loan on a 10-unit property, he assumed his strong credit and down payment would guarantee approval, but the lender wasn't just evaluating him — they were evaluating the property's income performance.

The deal fell short because its DSCR was 1.0, meaning income only met the loan obligation with no safety margin. Lenders typically require 1.20.

Instead of giving up, DeShawn worked with his real estate advisor to identify small rent increases and operational efficiencies that improved NOI. With those changes in place, he reapplied — and was approved.

When the numbers work, the deal works.

▧ **Cross-Reference:** *For expanded examples and templates, see Chapter 5 — "Strategic Deal Analysis: Turning Numbers into Narrative.*

Develop Your Pitch

Your message is your magnet

In multifamily real estate, your pitch is more than an introduction — it's your positioning. It tells clients who you serve, what you deliver, and why you're the advisor they should trust.

A strong pitch doesn't chase attention; it **commands clarity.**

It instantly communicates your value in a way that separates you from generalists and signals that you understand the complexity of multifamily investing.

Every multifamily advisor needs a clear value statement:

"I help [**target client**] achieve [**desired result**] by [**unique method**]."

This framework does three things:

- Identifies exactly who you serve
- Clarifies what measurable benefit you provide
- Highlights how you deliver it differently

Example:

"I help new investors achieve steady cash flow through small apartment acquisitions and smart financing strategies."

This statement tells a client what to expect and creates immediate alignment — especially when speaking with investors who value clarity and efficiency.

Your pitch should feel natural, confident, and consistent. **Whether you're:**

- **Introducing yourself at an investor meetup**
- **Posting on social media**
- **Emailing a new lead**
- **Speaking with a lender**
- **Reviewing a property with a client**

Your value statement becomes the through-line of your brand.

Practice it until it becomes the way you introduce your value everywhere you go.

When you communicate with precision, clients know instantly that you operate with purpose — and they trust you faster.

Adopt Data-Driven Decision Making

Facts create focus — and in multifamily real estate, focus determines momentum.

While emotions fluctuate daily, data provides the stability and clarity needed to make consistent, strategic decisions.

Top-performing advisors don't guess their way to success.
They **measure** their way there.

Track:

- Number of investor conversations weekly — reveals whether you're building meaningful pipeline volume

- Offers submitted vs. accepted — indicates deal competitiveness and pricing accuracy
- Lead sources that convert — shows where your marketing is actually working
- Follow-up frequency and response times — exposes gaps in your communication rhythm

These simple metrics create a truth-based view of your business — not one based on feeling busy, overwhelmed, or inconsistent.

Data reveals patterns that emotions overlook.

It shows:

- Where your strongest clients come from
- Which conversations lead to offers
- Which follow-up habits create the highest returns
- Where time is being wasted
- When the market is shifting before headlines catch up

With data, you stop reacting and start engineering better outcomes.

Let measurable insight — not momentum or mood — determine where you invest your energy.

When you track your actions, your actions become intentional — And intentional action compounds into mastery.

Establish Consistency Rituals

Discipline turns motion into momentum.

Success in multifamily real estate isn't built on intensity — it's built on consistency.

The advisor who shows up with small, repeated actions will outperform the advisor who works in occasional bursts of effort.

Consistency rituals create structure, stability, and predictability in a business that can feel unpredictable.

Set non-negotiables:

- Two hours of prospecting daily — keeps your pipeline active and prevents income droughts
- Weekly market review — ensures you stay aligned with shifts in pricing, demand, and investor sentiment
- Monthly investor meetups — expands your network and keeps you visible in the investment community
- Quarterly goal evaluation — realigns your systems with your long-term vision and corrects course when needed

These rituals are not tasks — they're commitments to your future self.

Consistency compounds.

Each routine you protect becomes a brick in your reputation — the architecture that supports your credibility, your client relationships, and your long-term success.

Clients trust advisors who are predictable, prepared, and present.

When your rituals are consistent, your presence in the market becomes consistent — and consistency is the foundation of confidence.

Stay Coachable

Humility is a profit multiplier.

In multifamily real estate, the most valuable advisors are not the ones who know everything — they are the ones committed to continuous learning.

The market evolves quickly, and those who refuse to evolve with it eventually fall behind.

Interest rates shift.

Lending standards tighten or loosen.

Tenant laws change.

Tax strategies adapt to new economic cycles.

What worked last year may not work this year — and what works today may look different six months from now.

Staying coachable means remaining open to new information, new strategies, and new perspectives.

It requires a willingness to ask questions, seek clarity, and refine your approach even when you feel confident.

Stay connected to mentors, peers, and environments that challenge your thinking and expand your skill set.

Surround yourself with people who:

- Push you intellectually
- Spot blind spots before they become liabilities
- Offer insight from real-world experience
- Hold you accountable to your goals

A coachable advisor stays relevant, resilient, and ready for what's next.

They adapt quickly, absorb information faster, and make better decisions because they understand that growth is a lifelong responsibility — not a one-time accomplishment.

Reflection Prompt

(Pause and consider before moving forward.)

- Which foundational principle resonates most with your current growth stage?
- How can you integrate it into your daily practice this week?

YOU BELONG HERE

Imposter syndrome is the enemy of progress.

Every expert you admire once stood exactly where you stand now — learning, questioning, refining.

The difference is simply that they kept going.

You have earned your place in this industry, and your growth will one day give others the confidence to begin their own journey.

Growth begins the moment you decide to continue.

What's Next

You've learned to position yourself as a multifamily strategist — fluent in the language, confident in the process, and grounded in purpose.

In the next chapter, we'll take these foundations and translate them into strategy — analyzing deals like an investor, not just selling them as an agent.

Prepare to see the numbers tell the story.

Chapter 4 — Developing an Investor's Mindset

In real estate, success begins long before you sign a listing agreement or tour a property.

It begins with perspective — the way you think, interpret, and respond to opportunities.

An agent without an investor's mindset sells transactions.

An agent with an investor's mindset builds wealth — not just for clients, but for themselves.

Understanding the Investor's Lens

The investor's mindset is rooted in value, not vanity.

Where most agents see listings, investors see leverage — opportunities to create income, reduce inefficiencies, and amplify returns.

Investors evaluate properties through a financial lens, not an emotional one. They look beyond curb appeal and ask the deeper, more strategic question:

"How can this property maximize its potential?"

This shift in thinking is what separates top-producing multifamily advisors from average residential ones. Residential agents often focus on aesthetics — finishes, light fixtures, paint colors, and the emotional appeal of the space. Investors focus on performance — the income engine that powers the property.

Understanding this distinction is crucial for your growth as a multifamily advisor because your clients expect you to think like them.

They expect you to interpret:

- Weaknesses as opportunities
- Problems as potential value

- Inefficiencies as upside
- Market movement as timing

To develop this mindset, train yourself to look past appearances and observe the operational reality. A property with peeling paint, outdated flooring, or aging appliances may look unattractive — but to an investor, it may be underperforming, not undesirable.

Underperformance is where value is created — That is the investor's lens.

Numbers tell stories — about efficiency, potential, and sustainability.

They reveal whether a property is thriving, struggling, or simply stagnant.

They expose mismanagement, hidden value, and unrealized opportunity.

Learn to read those stories like a language.

The more fluent you become, the more investors trust you — because you are no longer describing properties; you are decoding them.

"An investor doesn't ask what a property looks like; they ask what it earns."

And once you understand how to see through that lens, you stop walking buildings — and start reading them.

Trade Emotions for Evaluation

Most people buy with emotions and justify with logic.
Investors reverse that order.

They lead with numbers and allow emotions to validate — not dictate — the decision.

This distinction is foundational in multifamily real estate because it determines how clearly you can assess opportunity, risk, and value.

When you approach a property with emotional neutrality, you see it the way an investor does:
not as it feels, but as it functions.

Emotions can blur judgment.

Excitement can inflate perceived value.

Aesthetic appeal can distract from operational weaknesses.

Evaluation, however, brings clarity.

When you walk a property, practice shifting from emotional reactions to strategic observation. Instead of falling in love with finishes or charm, train yourself to look beneath the surface and ask:

- What's the current cash flow?
- What's the vacancy rate?
- Are there hidden expenses or deferred maintenance?
- What's the upside through rent optimization or repositioning?

These questions anchor you in performance, not perception.

This doesn't make the process cold or unfeeling — it makes it intentional.

Investors still care about community, stability, and quality of life, but they prioritize long-term sustainability over short-term sparkle.

When your clients see you lead with facts instead of flattery — with insight instead of enthusiasm — your credibility multiplies.

You become the advisor who protects their interests, sharpens their decisions, and sees what others overlook.

This is how trust is built in the multifamily space — through clarity, confidence, and a commitment to truth over temptation

FIELD INSIGHT — Tasha's Shift from Emotion to Evaluation

Tasha was a residential agent turned multifamily specialist.

She realized her language was still rooted in single-family emotions — "beautiful," "cozy," "great natural light."

Her investor clients were polite, but uninterested.

After shadowing a seasoned broker, she learned to speak in numbers: "8% cap rate," "5% below market rents,", "projected NOI growth."

Within months, her confidence — and her commission volume tripled.

— From the author's field notes

Ownership Thinking

An investor's mindset begins with ownership — not owning property, but understanding how owners think, operate, and make decisions.

As an agent, adopting this perspective allows you to guide clients with greater precision, clarity, and long-term vision.

Ownership thinking is the mindset shift that transforms an agent into an advisor.

It moves you from simply participating in a transaction to guiding the long-term financial trajectory of your clients.

When you think like an owner, you:

- Protect time like capital
  You stop giving energy to distractions, low-quality leads, and chaotic workflows.
  You begin treating your time as a resource with return on investment.
- Treat relationships like assets
  Every connection — lenders, brokers, property managers, investors — becomes part of an ecosystem you nurture intentionally.
  Owners know that relationships compound like capital.
- Approach learning like due diligence
  You evaluate information with curiosity and precision rather than passively consuming it.

Owners learn with purpose because every insight shapes future decisions.

Ownership thinking gives you emotional distance and strategic clarity.

Instead of reacting to the market, your clients, or your workload, you begin forecasting — anticipating needs, identifying patterns, and positioning yourself ahead of challenges.

This mindset also anchors your confidence.

When you see yourself as a steward of value — not a seller of property — you elevate the way you communicate, negotiate, and advise.

You become the person investors rely on not just for deals, but for direction.

Ownership thinking is the bridge between "agent" and "authority."
It's where leadership begins.

Terms Every Multifamily Real Estate Advisor Should Know

To communicate effectively with investors, you must speak the language of multifamily income, operations, value, and financing.

These terms are the foundation of credibility. Advisors who understand them — not superficially, but conceptually — immediately gain trust, authority, and influence.

Here are the core terms every multifamily agent-advisor must master, organized for clarity and professional readiness.

Income & Revenue Terms

◆ **PGI (Potential Gross Income)**

What it is:

The total income a property could generate at full occupancy and market rents.

Why it Matters:

Reveals income potential and identifies under-market rents and missed revenue opportunities.

◆ **Vacancy & Credit Loss**

What it is:

Income lost to vacant units, late payments, and non-payment.

Why it Matters:

Shows whether a building has demand issues or management weaknesses.

◆ **EGI (Effective Gross Income)**

What it is:

The actual income the property earns after subtracting vacancy and adding ancillary income.

Why it Matters:

Reflects real performance — not projections or assumptions.

◆ **Other Income / Ancillary Income**

What it is:

Non-rent income such as parking, storage, laundry, pet fees, RUBS, and admin fees.

Why it Matters:

A key driver of value-add potential; advisors use it to show investors where easy upside exists.

Operating Performance Terms

◆ **NOI (Net Operating Income)**

What it is:

Income after subtracting operating expenses from EGI.

Why it Matters:

Determines value, financing, risk, and long-term stability.
NOI is the heartbeat of multifamily.

◆ **Operating Expense Ratio (OER)**

What it is:

Total operating expenses ÷ EGI.

Why it Matters:

Shows efficiency. High OER signals cost issues; low OER may signal under-maintenance.

◆ **Economic Occupancy**

What it is:

The percentage of income collected vs. income expected at full occupancy.

Why it Matters:

A property can be physically full but financially weak. Advisors must know the difference.

Value & Return Terms

◆ **Cap Rate**

What it is:

NOI ÷ Purchase Price — a quick measure of return relative to price.

Why it Matters:

Used to compare deals, understand market expectations, and evaluate value.

◆ **Cash-on-Cash Return**

What it is:

Annual pre-tax cash flow ÷ total cash invested.

Why it Matters:

Shows investors how hard their money is working in real time.

◆ **Breakeven Occupancy**

What it is:

The occupancy percentage needed to cover all expenses and debt service.

Why it Matters:

Reveals how resilient a property is to market downturns or leasing challenges.

◆ **Repositioning**

What it is:

Strategically improving units or operations to increase income and value.

Why it Matters:

Signals forced appreciation opportunities — one of the biggest investor decision drivers.

Financing & Lending Terms

◆ **DSCR (Debt Service Coverage Ratio)**

What it is:

NOI ÷ Annual Debt Service.

Why it Matters:
Shows the property's ability to pay its mortgage.
Lenders require 1.20+ in most markets.

◆ **LTV (Loan-to-Value Ratio)**
What it is:
Loan amount ÷ property value.

Why it Matters:
Impacts down payments, interest rates, and financing approval.

◆ **Interest-Only Periods**
What it is:
Periods where borrowers pay only interest, not principal.

Why it Matters:
Boosts early cash flow and investor returns — advisors should recognize when it's beneficial.

◆ **Amortization Schedule**
What it is:
Breakdown of principal vs. interest payments over time.

Why it Matters:
Affects cash flow, long-term cost, and refinancing strategy.

Essential Documents & Analysis Tools

◆ **Rent Roll**
What it is:
A line-by-line record of unit rents, lease terms, deposits, and concessions.

Why it Matters:
Shows income strength, stability of tenants, and future rent projections.

◆ T-12 (Trailing 12-Month Financials)
What it is:
The past 12 months of income and expenses.

Why it Matters:
The single most important document in underwriting.
Reveals true performance — not estimates.

◆ Pro Forma
What it is:
Projected future financial performance based on assumptions.

Why it Matters:
Used to evaluate value-add potential and guide investor strategy.

Seeing Property Through an Investor's Lens

Before you learn to calculate performance metrics, you must understand why investors depend on them.

In multifamily real estate, numbers are not simply data points — they are behavioral indicators. They reveal how a property performs under real conditions, how stable it is, and how much potential it holds for growth.

Investors don't evaluate buildings based on how they look.
They evaluate them based on how they behave.

A property is a living financial ecosystem. Its income patterns, turnover rates, tenant behaviors, and operational efficiencies tell a story — sometimes of strength, sometimes of struggle, sometimes of hidden opportunity.

Your job as an advisor is to interpret that story before you ever open a spreadsheet.

What It Means to See Like an Investor

Developing an investor's lens means retraining your eyes to focus on the financial signals behind the physical structure.

As you walk or research properties in your market, begin noticing:

- What story do the rents tell?

- ◆ Does the building appear well-managed or neglected?
- ◆ Is occupancy consistent in the surrounding area?
- ◆ Do the units reflect their full market potential?
- ◆ Where might value be hidden or underutilized?

Investors win by identifying opportunities others overlook.

➢ ***Keynote:***

When you begin to see properties through this lens:

- You identify upside faster
- You recommend strategies with clarity
- You build credibility before the numbers even appear

— Mindset before math. Perspective before performance.

You are not calculating yet — that comes in Chapter 7.
Right now, you are building the instinct investors rely on.

How You Know You're Beginning to Think Like an Investor

An investor's mindset develops through repetition, exposure, and disciplined observation. You'll know the shift is taking place when your instincts begin to change — often before your confidence fully catches up.

You may notice that:

- ◆ You ask about NOI before finishes or aesthetics
- ◆ You naturally identify rent gaps and operational inefficiencies
- ◆ You think in scenarios rather than guarantees
- ◆ You speak in ranges, risks, and trade-offs — not absolutes
- ◆ You evaluate opportunities based on long-term behavior, not immediate appeal

These are early indicators of investor fluency. They signal that your perspective is expanding beyond transactions and into value interpretation — the skill investors rely on most when choosing their advisors.

Long-Term Vision Creates Long-Term Wealth

Most real estate advisors focus on the next transaction. Investors focus on the next decade.

This difference in perspective is what separates short-term activity from long-term prosperity.

In multifamily real estate, the advisors who adopt an investor's time horizon build careers that are more stable, more strategic, and more financially rewarding.

A long-term vision shapes how you evaluate deals, nurture relationships, and develop your own expertise. It turns your business into an asset — not a job.

Short-Term Mindset vs. Investor Mindset

Many agents chase fast wins:

- quick listings
- quick closings
- quick commission checks
- quick recognition

But these wins fade as quickly as they appear.

Investors think differently. They are willing to trade immediate comfort for future growth.

This shift—from urgency to patience—is the line between transactions and wealth creation.

Long-Term Thinking Increases Your Income — It Doesn't Postpone It

Adopting a long-term mindset strengthens your pipeline, improves the quality of your clients, and increases the financial impact of each transaction.

This is not about delaying earnings. This is about increasing them — intelligently and sustainably.

💼 **In Practice — What Long-Term Thinking Looks Like**

When you begin to think like an investor, your daily actions shift in subtle but powerful ways.

You stop chasing transactions and start building relationships that compound over time.

Legacy replaces limelight.
Substance replaces speed.
Quality replaces urgency.

You are no longer operating deal to deal — you are operating as a strategist with direction, clarity, and purpose.

Reflection Point

(Pause and consider before moving forward.)

Where in your current practice are you still thinking like a salesperson instead of an investor?

How would your conversations, priorities, or daily decisions change if you evaluated opportunities through an ownership mindset rather than a transactional one?

What's Next

Now that you understand the foundation of multifamily real estate sales, it's time to rise above the basics — to think, act, and build like a true multifamily real estate advisor.

The investor's mindset looks for performance, not prettiness.

- Numbers build trust; emotions build attachment.
- Learn to evaluate, calculate, and communicate like an investor.
- Think like an owner so you can advise owners effectively.

Now that you've learned to **see** like an investor, the next chapter teaches you how to **analyze** like one — where numbers meet negotiation and vision becomes valuation.

— ***Time to Elevate***

PART II

PROFESSIONAL PRACTICE

Purpose becomes progress only when it is practiced.

In Part I, you established clarity — why multifamily real estate matters, how your mindset must shift, and where you belong within this industry

But understanding alone does not build a career.

Confidence is forged through repetition, structure, and disciplined execution.

Part II is where intention turns into professional practice.

Here, you begin translating belief into behavior. You will learn how to prospect with purpose, communicate with authority, and build systems that support consistency rather than relying on motivation alone.

This section focuses on the daily mechanics of becoming a trusted multifamily advisor — not through hustle, but through alignment, preparation, and strategic presence.

Professional practice is not about doing more. It is about doing the right things, repeatedly, with clarity and restraint.

These chapters are designed to help you:

- Build a sustainable pipeline rooted in strategy rather than urgency
- Develop communication habits that establish credibility and trust
- Show up prepared, confident, and positioned — even when you are still growing

This is where discipline replaces doubt. Where habits replace hesitation. Where your professional identity begins to solidify.

You are no longer asking if you belong. Now, you are learning how to operate.

Let's begin.

Chapter 5 — Building Your Pipeline and Prospecting Like A Pro

A consistent pipeline is the heartbeat of every successful agent's business

Without it, income becomes unpredictable, motivation fades, and fear takes over.

With it, momentum builds — confidence rises, opportunities multiply, and success becomes measurable.

Multifamily real estate is a numbers-driven industry, but not in the simplistic way most agents imagine.

It's about building relationships systematically and nurturing them with intention.
Prospecting isn't begging for business — it's positioning yourself as a solution.

Activity Over Anxiety

Prospecting is not merely an action — it is a discipline.

In multifamily real estate, the advisors who consistently outperform others aren't the loudest or the luckiest; they are the most intentional.

Your emotional stability, deal flow, and confidence all rise from one source: **controlled activity done with purpose.**

When your pipeline is full, you operate from confidence instead of desperation.

The anxiety of *"not knowing where the next deal will come from"* is usually the byproduct of inconsistent, reactive outreach.

Activity cures anxiety.

Schedule prospecting with the same seriousness you bring to closings.

Protect those hours with discipline. Pipeline maintenance is not optional — it is the engine of your entire career.

Define Your Prospecting Goals

Precision begins with clarity.

A strong pipeline isn't built on hustle alone — it is built on measurable, focused output.

When you set defined targets, prospecting shifts from guesswork to guidance and from overwhelm to control.

But beyond structure, goals transform the *psychology* of your business.

Goals eliminate emotional decision-making.

They replace uncertainty with direction.

They transform a scattered workday into a strategic plan.

When you define your prospecting goals clearly, three powerful things occur:

1. You reclaim control of your outcomes.

Without goals, prospecting becomes reactive — based on mood, energy, or fear.

With goals, every outreach, follow-up, and conversation has purpose.

You move from *"I hope business shows up"* to *"I created opportunities today."*

2. Your consistency becomes measurable, not accidental.

Most agents don't have a pipeline problem — they have a measurement problem.

When you know exactly what you're aiming for, you can see whether you are on track, drifting, or outperforming.

Measurement builds confidence because progress becomes visible.

3. You begin thinking like an advisor, not a salesperson.

Investors operate from benchmarks, ratios, and targets.

When you adopt the same disciplined approach, your conversations naturally become more strategic, more confident, and more credible.

Set specific, trackable objectives such as:

- 25 outreach calls per week to property owners or investors
- 10 follow-up emails to warm prospects
- 5 new investors added to your CRM (Customer Relationship Management) system weekly
- 2 property tours monthly with qualified clients

Write these goals down and review them weekly.

Your progress becomes easier to track, your conversations become more strategic, and your business becomes a measurable system rather than a series of hopeful attempts.

Goals create direction; measurement creates momentum.

And when every action is tied to a measurable outcome, your entire business gains structure, focus, and predictability — the hallmarks of a true advisor.

Segment Your Prospect List

Prioritization is a leadership skill.

In multifamily real estate, not every relationship carries the same weight — and the advisors who learn to sort opportunities with intention gain clarity faster than those who treat every lead the same.

Segmentation is more than organization; it is strategic allocation.

It ensures your time, energy, and expertise flow toward the relationships most likely to convert, mature, or become long-term advisory clients.

When you learn to segment your pipeline, three things happen:

1. Your time becomes an asset, not a reaction.
Without segmentation, advisors spend equal effort on unequal opportunities.

With segmentation, your calendar reflects your priorities — not your distractions.

2. Your follow-up becomes purposeful, not mechanical.

Different clients require different conversations, touchpoints, insights, and cadence.

Segmentation gives you the clarity to show up with relevance, not noise.

3. Your results become predictable instead of sporadic.

Because you're investing energy into prospects with the highest likelihood of movement — not the loudest voices or most convenient contacts.

Strategy begins with sorting your priorities.

Categorize your database into clear tiers:

Tier 1 — Warm

Active investors, hot buyers, or immediate sellers.

These are your highest-probability clients — they require consistent communication, tailored opportunities, and timely action.

Tier 2 — Nurture

Interested prospects who are not yet ready to transact.

These relationships grow through education, steady guidance, market updates, and regular value-driven touchpoints.

Tier 3 — Cold

Long-term relationships, casual connections, or prospects with distant timelines.

These individuals benefit from newsletters, general market reports, event invitations, and low-pressure communication.

Tailor your follow-up accordingly:

- Warm leads need consistent, focused check-ins.
- Nurture leads need education and insight.
- Cold leads need presence without pressure.

This simple discipline turns your prospect list into a functional system rather than an unstructured collection of names.

Segmentation is the quiet foundation of advisory-level prospecting — it ensures that every action you take has intention, and every relationship you invest in has purpose.

▧ **Cross-Reference:** *For deeper insight on building client archetypes, see Chapter 7 — "Client Profiling and Negotiation Strategy."*

Locating Property Owners and Decision Makers

Before an advisor can offer insight, they must establish contact with the right person.

In multifamily real estate, information is leverage — and knowing who actually controls a property is the first step in building meaningful advisory relationships.

This isn't random cold calling.

This is intentional, research-based outreach that positions you as a professional who brings clarity, not noise.

Establishing ownership correctly matters because:

- It prevents wasted time.
  You avoid chasing wrong numbers, uninvolved contacts, or outdated records.
- It accelerates credibility.
  Decision-makers immediately recognize when you've done your homework.
- It sets you apart from average agents.
  Most agents rely on guesswork. Advisors rely on verified information.

Below is the advisory-level process used by professional multifamily brokers, top producers, and commercial analysts:

How to Correctly Identify and Document Ownership

1. Start with the tax record

- Search the property in the county tax database
- Identify whether the owner is an individual, an LLC, a trust, or a corporate entity

Why it matters:

Tax records are the most reliable starting point because they reflect *legal ownership*, not hearsay or assumption.

2. If an LLC is listed, search the business registration

Use the state's Secretary of State website to identify:

– Registered agents
– Managers or managing members
– Contact information on file

Why it matters:

LLCs often mask the real decision-maker.
Finding the managing member reveals **who actually makes financial decisions**, not just who receives mail.

3. Cross-reference with professional tools

Platforms such as Reonomy, PropertyRadar, or CoStar can confirm:

– Ownership structure
– Portfolio size
– Mailing addresses
– Associated contacts

Why it matters:

Professional tools help verify accuracy, reveal deeper owner insights, and show whether the owner holds multiple properties (increasing future opportunity).

4. Document accurately in your CRM

Create or update the ownership record with:

– Legal owner
– Key decision-makers
– Verified contact details
– Preferred communication notes
– Portfolio indicators (unit count, submarkets, asset class)

Why it matters:
A CRM is your advisory memory.

Accurate documentation ensures every future touch-point is informed, relevant, and precise.

5. Ensure compliance and professionalism

- Follow local privacy, marketing, and contact-permission laws
- Avoid unauthorized scraping tools
- Treat ownership research as confidential intelligence

Why it matters:
Professionalism protects your reputation and positions you as a trusted industry resource — not a spammer or opportunist.

➢ ***Keynote:***

Identifying the correct owner is not busywork —
it is foundational to professional outreach.

When you contact the right person with the right insight, your credibility accelerates instantly.

You are no longer *"another agent calling."*

You become the advisor who:

- Knows who owns what
- Understands their investment patterns
- Identifies opportunity early
- Respects their time
- Brings value before asking for anything

This single discipline separates the causal agent from the multifamily professional.

Leverage Data and Technology

Systems amplify skill.

In real estate, technology is not optional — it is the infrastructure that supports consistency, accuracy, and professional credibility.

Your ability to track relationships, interpret market shifts, and follow up strategically depends on the quality of your systems and the discipline with which you use them.

Advisors who embrace technology scale faster, communicate smarter, and operate with greater clarity.

Those who resist it remain limited by memory, momentum, and manual effort — all of which eventually fail under the pressure of a growing business.

Your **CRM**, research tools, and data platforms are not administrative conveniences — they are your **revenue infrastructure**.

A CRM is more than a digital contact list.

It is your chronological record of every conversation, every promise made, every follow-up scheduled, and every investor preference identified.

It becomes the institutional memory of your business — the safeguard that prevents details from slipping, opportunities from fading, and relationships from stalling.

Use it to track:

- Touchpoints
- Follow-up cycles
- Investor goals
- Property interests
- Renewal reminders
- Decision-maker intelligence
- Anniversaries

These details matter because investors value advisors who remember the specifics — the last conversation, their preferred asset class, their timeline, their concerns, their goals.

Technology enables you to operate with that level of precision even as your pipeline expands.

Automate reminders to ensure nothing slips through the cracks.

Templates maintain tone and consistency.

Tags help you deliver targeted communication at the right moment to the right clients.

Technology does not replace your expertise — **it amplifies it**.

It allows you to show up reliably, professionally, and strategically, even on the busiest days.

In multifamily real estate, where relationships deepen over months and opportunities surface unexpectedly, a strong technology system is not a luxury — it is a competitive advantage.

Using AI as a Prospecting and CRM Enhancement Tool

AI is not a replacement for expertise — it is an efficiency amplifier.

In multifamily real estate, where timing, clarity, and consistency drive opportunity, AI can support your workflow without ever replacing the human judgment clients depend on.

Think of AI as a silent operations partner.

It strengthens discipline, sharpens communication, and reduces administrative drag so you can spend more time advising and less time chasing tasks.

◆ Drafting and Polishing Communication

AI can help refine emails, follow-up scripts, outreach templates, and market updates so your message is clear and confident.

A polished message builds immediate credibility when prospecting owners or investors.

◆ **Enhancing CRM Organization and Consistency**

AI can support CRM workflows by helping you:

- summarize previous conversations
- categorize leads based on behavior
- identify optimal follow-up timing
- add tailored notes that improve personalization

Your CRM becomes a living intelligence system — not a static database.

◆ **Research Support and Market Interpretation**

AI can summarize market reports, rental trend publications, and economic updates, allowing you to grasp insights faster while you still verify accuracy.

◆ **Building Prospecting Scripts and Call Frameworks**

AI assists with:

- outreach scripts
- voicemail templates
- objection-handling guidance
- educational explanations for new investors

You keep your voice — AI sharpens the delivery.

◆ **Supporting Value-Based Touchpoints**

AI can create first drafts for:

- market snapshots
- newsletter outlines
- social media educational posts
- investor resource sheets

You refine and finalize them to match your tone.

➢ ***Keynote:***

AI enhances your systems, but your insight builds trust.
Used wisely, AI increases consistency, clarity, and professional presence.

Build a Daily Prospecting Routine

Structure eliminates resistance. Rhythm builds revenue.

A predictable routine is not merely helpful — it is transformative.

When your days follow a deliberate pattern, your results become measurable, your confidence stabilizes, and your pipeline evolves from chaotic to controlled.

A high-performing advisor does not wake up wondering where to begin.

They follow a cadence that compounds. Their routines act as a safety net that prevents slow months, protects against burnout, and ensures that revenue momentum never stalls.

Craft a routine that reinforces momentum:

- **Monday — Owner Outreach & New Investor Calls**
  Begin the week by initiating conversations, not waiting for them
  Momentum established early carries through the week.

- **Tuesday — Follow-Ups & Warm Touchpoints**
  Revisit conversations from the previous week and move relationships forward.
  Deals are rarely won in the first call — they are won in the follow-up.

- **Wednesday — Property Research & Market Intelligence**
  Analyze active listings, rental trends, and recent closings.
  Research days sharpen your advisory insight and keep your language investor-focused.

- **Thursday — Networking Calls & Event Engagement**
  Strengthen your professional circle.
  Investors, lenders, property managers, and contractors all shape your deal flow and market clarity.

- **Friday — Pipeline Review & Weekend Preparation**
  Assess progress, adjust priorities, and close loops.
  A clean pipeline heading into the weekend creates mental clarity and reduces stress.

This rhythm creates predictability. Predictability creates peace. And peace frees you to operate from strategy instead of survival.

A daily prospecting routine is not about doing more — it is about doing what matters most with disciplined consistency.

APPLIED APPLICATION — The Prospecting Conversation Flow

A powerful conversation is both strategic and human.

This framework helps you lead with value, uncover intent, and guide the dialogue without pressure — a hallmark of professional advisory communication.

Practical Flow for Meaningful Engagement

1. Warm Greeting — personalize your approach

("I noticed your building on Peachtree and wanted to share a quick update…")

Tailored openings disarm skepticism and build immediate rapport.

2. Value Opener — offer quick insight

("Cap rates have shifted about 0.5% this quarter…")

Begin with information that positions you as a resource, not a salesperson.

3. Discovery Question — identify their motivation or challenge

Ask what matters most to them.

Insight sharpens your ability to deliver relevant value.

4. Resource Offer — provide something useful and immediate

Share a brief report, update, or data point that aligns with their goals or concerns.

Value given early builds trust quickly.

5. Next Step — establish momentum with clarity

Book a follow-up call or send curated information tailored to their situation.

Clear next steps prevent the conversation from losing energy.

This conversational rhythm creates connection without pressure.

It allows the other party to experience your professionalism — and trust your expertise — before ever being asked for commitment.

➢ ***Keynote:***

The Two-Hour Rule of Momentum

Dedicated prospecting time compounds results faster than any marketing tactic.

The advisors who win are not the ones who try the hardest, but the ones who show up the most consistently.

Guard this daily window with the same seriousness you'd give a closing. Discipline is a profit engine.

Adopt the "Give First" Strategy

Value precedes opportunity.

In multifamily real estate, authority is built long before a client signs a listing agreement or schedules a tour — it is built the moment you demonstrate insight without expecting anything in return.

Most agents lead with requests. Advisors lead with relevance.

Instead of asking,

"Do you have any properties to sell?"
ask,

"Would you like a quick market update on multifamily performance in your area?"

One approach demands something. The other provides something.

Giving value first — whether through data, analysis, perspective, or market intelligence — positions you as a trusted advisor rather than a transactional seeker.

Education is a differentiator. Insight is a magnet.

Every "*give*" strengthens your authority. Every "ask" should follow value.

Leading with generosity is not soft — it is strategic.

In an industry driven by trust, the advisor who teaches becomes the advisor who earns the business.

APPLIED APLICATION — MARKET REPORTS AND NEWSLETTERS

Advisors who consistently share clear, relevant market insight quickly become recognized as credible voices in their market.

A simple, polished market update helps you develop your analytical instincts and positions you as a resource for both owners and investors.

This exercise strengthens your ability to observe and interpret the larger patterns shaping your local multifamily landscape.

How to create a clean, high-impact market snapshot

1. Gather current multifamily market data from reliable sources

Use platforms such as

- MLS
- LoopNet
- CoStar
- CREXI
- CBRE and Marcus & Millichap reports
  Yardi Matrix or similar rental trend publications

From these sources, identify:

- Reported cap-rate ranges
- Noted rental movement (increasing, stabilizing, or softening)
- Recent sales worth observing
- Active listings representing potential opportunity

2. Create a simple, branded one-page snapshot

Use tools such as Canva or Adobe Express. Include:

Your logo and professional branding

- A clear headline ("Multifamily Market Snapshot — [City/Quarter]")
- Three to five key data highlights
- Simple callouts or minimal graphics to keep the design polished

3. Add a brief interpretation paragraph

Offer a concise, thoughtful perspective, such as:

- *"Recent trades suggest strong investor confidence in the northeast submarket."*
- *"Rent growth has stabilized, signaling potential opportunities for value-add repositioning."*

This helps you practice translating data into meaningful narrative.

4. Include a "Top 3 Opportunities to Watch" section

These are not analyzed deals — they are curated observations:

- A stable asset showing consistent occupancy
- A building in an emerging rental corridor
- A listing with visible value-add potential

5. Send your snapshot monthly to your sphere

Consistency builds recognition.

Professional rhythm builds reputation.

Readers will begin associating you with clarity, intelligence, and steady guidance.

▧ **Cross-Reference:** *In Chapter 6 — "Strategic Deal Analysis," you'll learn how to convert observed market data into deeper advisory conversations.*

Remember, persistence without empathy becomes pressure.

Great advisors read tone, timing, and temperament — they listen for opportunity rather than chase it.

Tracking Metrics That Matter

Activity creates motion — but metrics create mastery.

Numbers are more than tallies; they are teachers.
They reveal patterns you cannot feel, expose weaknesses you may not notice, and illuminate opportunities long before intuition can.

Most agents measure effort.

Advisors measure effectiveness.

Metrics shift your business from emotional interpretation (*"I think I'm doing okay"*) to empirical clarity (*"I know exactly what's working and what isn't"*).

They turn your pipeline into an observable, predictable system — one you can refine, optimize, and scale with intention.

Beyond counting calls or emails, track the indicators that actually reflect your influence:

◆ **Conversation-to-Meeting Ratio**

What it measures:

How many initial conversations convert into scheduled appointments.

Why it matters:

This reveals the strength of your introduction, the clarity of your value proposition, and the level of trust you can establish quickly.

High ratios equal strong positioning; low ratios signal messaging gaps.

◆ **Meeting-to-Opportunity Ratio**

What it measures:

The percentage of meetings that advance into real opportunities.

Why it matters:

It shows whether your communication aligns with investor priorities.

If relationships stall after the meeting stage, your advisory framing — not your skill — may need refinement.

◆ **Proposal-to-Close Ratio**

What it measures:

Of the proposals or analyses you deliver; how many become signed agreements or offers?

Why it matters:

This ratio reveals the precision of your recommendations, your ability to align solutions with client goals, and the overall effectiveness of your advisory approach.

◆ **Lead Source Conversions**

What it measures:

Which channels consistently produce engaged, high-quality prospects.

Why it matters:

Every market is different. These insights help you invest time and resources where the results are strongest — and pull away from the channels that drain energy without producing return.

◆ **Average Response Time**

What it measures:

How quickly you follow up when someone expresses interest or asks a question.

Why it matters:

Speed communicates professionalism.

In commercial real estate, responsiveness often determines whether a buyer selects *you* or moves on to someone else.

These micro-metrics reveal not just how often you show up, but how effectively you connect.

They turn your pipeline into a measurable ecosystem — one that evolves with your career and strengthens every time you evaluate it.

Mastery is not built by activity alone.
It is built by what you choose to measure, study, and adjust.

Measure, Adjust, and Repeat

Data doesn't judge — it directs.

At the end of each week, your metrics reveal the truth about your performance: what is working, what is stalling, and where your energy is producing real traction.

Advisors who grow consistently are those who pause long enough to study their own patterns.

Ask yourself:

- **How many new leads were added?**
  Growth begins with expansion.
  If the top of your funnel is thin, the rest of the pipeline will always feel unpredictable.
- **How many follow-ups were completed?**
  Follow-up is the quiet engine of conversion.
  Incomplete cycles signal where opportunities quietly die.
- **Which relationships advanced to the next stage?**
  Identify who moved from conversation • meeting • proposal • commitment.
- **Where did conversations stall or lose momentum?**
  Stalls reveal friction points — unclear value, weak positioning, or poor timing.

These are opportunities to refine language, adjust cadence, or strengthen relevance.

Use this data to fine-tune your approach each week.

Small adjustments compound, and disciplined review prevents your business from slipping into reactive mode.

Pipeline management is not a one-time setup — it is a living system that evolves as your business grows.

The more you measure, the more confidently you can lead.

Quality Conversations Drive Quality Results

Connection creates conversion — quality creates conversion.

You don't need hundreds of shallow interactions — you need consistent, meaningful conversations rooted in value, clarity, and genuine intent.

Every authentic engagement compounds over time.
Some seeds sprout immediately; others mature later.
But each touch builds familiarity, trust, and recognition.

In multifamily real estate, conversations are currency.

The advisor who cultivates real connection ultimately commands real opportunity.

When you focus on depth over volume, your pipeline becomes stronger, steadier, and more predictable.

> **FIELD INSIGHT — THE 90-DAY TURNAROUND**
>
> Carlos, a mid-level advisor stalled by slow closings, committed to one disciplined shift:
>
> *"Two hours of outreach daily — no excuses."*
>
> Within 90 days, he tripled his active client list and closed three multifamily deals.
>
> The work wasn't glamorous, but it was predictable — and predictability produced confidence, clarity, and peace.
>
> Consistency compounds. Discipline multiplies.

Reflection Point

(Pause and evaluate before you turn the page.)

How many quality conversations am I having each week?

- Do I have a system that ensures consistent follow-up?
- Where am I losing potential clients — at first contact, nurture, or close?
- What is one value-based outreach idea I can implement this month?

Your business grows in the areas you consistently examine.

What's Next

You've learned to build a consistent, strategic pipeline — one that replaces chaos with clarity and transforms prospecting into a disciplined, repeatable rhythm.

In the next chapter, we shift from relationship building to **analytical mastery** — understanding the numbers, narratives, and market forces that guide smart investment decisions.

Prepare to think like an investor and operate like a leader.

▩ LEADERSHIP CHALLENGE — FROM CONSISTENCY TO COMMAND

For the next 30 days, track every outreach touchpoint. Identify one behavioral adjustment — frequency, tone, or follow-through — that produced a measurable result.

Mastery begins when awareness meets data.

Chapter 6 — The Architecture of Communication Mastery

Real estate is a relationship business disguised as a sales business.

Client communication is not a collection of isolated skills — it is a progression.

Each principle in this chapter builds on the last, creating a layered foundation of mastery.

Trust opens the relationship.

Understanding deepens it.

Tone shapes how clients interpret your guidance.

Clarity helps them make informed decisions.

Empathy accelerates those decisions by addressing the root concerns.

Proactive communication prevents uncertainty before it appears.

Grace under pressure proves your leadership in difficult moments.

Retention systems maintain the relationship long after closing.

Loyalty becomes the natural result.

trust → understanding → communication → clarity → empathy → leadership → retention → loyalty.

Each concept elevates the next.
Each skill reinforces the others.

Together, they form the communication framework of a world-class multifamily advisor.

Trust Is Built in the Small Moments

Foundational principle — trust is the gateway to influence.

Trust is not earned in grand gestures — it is built in the quiet, consistent moments that signal reliability.

Clients decide whether they believe in you long before paperwork is signed and long before a financial decision is made.

Trust begins in:

- the first five minutes of a call
- the clarity of your emails
- the timeliness of your follow-up
- the steadiness of your tone during uncertainty

Professionalism is not about perfection — it is about predictability.

Clients want to know you will show up the same way every time: steady, informed, calm, and prepared.

In multifamily real estate, trust becomes leverage.

The advisor who earns it early gains influence later — during negotiations, during analysis, and during tense moments where buyers and sellers rely on your judgment.

"People don't choose the agent with the most expertise; they choose the agent whose expertise they trust."

Consistency builds familiarity.
Familiarity builds comfort.
Comfort builds confidence.

Trust is not an outcome — it is a strategy.

Adopt a Client-First Mindset

Perspective principle → understanding shapes how you communicate.

A client-first mindset is not about being agreeable — it is about being attuned.

Before every interaction, pause and ask yourself:

"What does this client need to feel confident right now?"

Confidence is the true currency of decision-making.

For some clients, confidence comes from clear numbers.
For others, it comes from calm reassurance.

And sometimes, confidence comes from giving them space — silence to think, process, or breathe.

Clients rarely say exactly what they need.

Your role is to interpret the moment, not dictate it.

A client-first mindset sounds like:

- *"Let me simplify that for you."*
- *"Take your time — I'm here when you're ready."*
- *"Would it help if I walked you through the financial side again?"*
- *"Here's what this means in everyday terms…"*

When you meet people where they truly are — emotionally, financially, and mentally — you shorten hesitations, deepen trust, and accelerate decisions.

Advisors who push lose clients.
Advisors who understand them keep them for life.

A client-first mindset is not soft.

It is strategic.

It is the foundation of every profitable relationship you will build in this industry.

Meet people where they are, not where you wish they were.

Tone Translation — How Words Shape Trust

Communication principle → how you speak becomes how clients experience you.

What you say matters, but *how* you say it determines whether clients feel steady, supported, and safe moving forward.

Tone Translation is the practice of choosing language that projects clarity, confidence, and calm.

Tone Translation = External phrasing (communication output)

It shapes the words clients hear — guiding them toward clarity instead of pressure.

Empathy Creates Efficiency = Internal interpretation (emotional input)

It shapes how you listen — interpreting hesitation, fear, or overwhelm before responding.

Together, they create a communication style that builds trust quickly and sustains it throughout the entire relationship.

Tone builds trust through expression.

Empathy sustains trust through interpretation.

Master both, and you transform dialogue into connection.

APPLIED APPLICATION —Tone Translation in Practice

Instead of saying:

> *"This deal will go fast — you need to act now."*

Say:

> *"This property is receiving interest. I want you to have the first, most informed opportunity to decide."*

One statement pressures. The other empowers.

Tone is not decoration — it is direction.

Your words can either create clarity or trigger hesitation.

Use language that reinforces trust.

Master Active Listening

Interpretive principle → listening reveals the insight that guides your strategy.

In multifamily advisory work, listening becomes your market intelligence.

Clients reveal their priorities, their fears, their timelines, and their decision-making patterns in the spaces between their words.

Your job is to catch the signals others miss.

Active listening is not waiting for your turn to speak — it is gathering insight.

It is paying attention to the words chosen, the tone expressed, and the emotion beneath the surface.

When clients speak, take notes.

Track keywords, preferences, hesitations, and any shift in tone.

Reflect what you hear before you offer guidance.

This reinforces clarity, reduces misunderstanding, and deepens trust.

When clients feel understood, they move decisively.

When they feel unheard, they hesitate.

APPLIED APPLICATION — Active Listening in Action

Use reflective language to confirm understanding and build rapport:

"So what I'm hearing is that stability and cash flow matter more to you than quick flips — is that right?"

This simple mirroring technique does three things simultaneously:

- It shows clients they are being heard.
- It clarifies their priorities before you advise.
- It builds trust faster than any scripted pitch ever could.

Listening is not a soft skill — it is a strategic one.

Master it, and every conversation becomes clearer, more efficient, and far more productive.

Simplify Complex Information

Clarity principle → simplification prepares clients to make confident decisions.

Multifamily clients often face an overwhelming flow of data — rent rolls, lease terms, expense structures, financing terms, and unfamiliar investment language.

When information feels heavy, decisions slow down.

Your role is not to impress them with jargon — it is to translate complexity into calm understanding.

A great advisor simplifies without diluting accuracy.

They turn abstract numbers into relatable meaning.

They explain without overwhelming.

They lead clients to insight rather than pushing them toward decisions

Use simple analogies and clear phrasing to anchor core concepts:

- *"Think of NOI as the property's paycheck — the amount it earns after covering its monthly responsibilities."*
- *"A cap rate works like the interest you earn on a savings account — it shows the return you get on what you pay."*
- *"Vacancy loss is the money the property didn't earn because units were empty or tenants didn't pay."*

When clients understand the language, they can participate in the strategy, and move forward with more confidence. When they feel lost, they withdraw or delay decisions.

This section prepares you to communicate value with accuracy and simplicity.

The deeper calculations and financial modeling come later in Chapter 7, when you'll learn how to interpret metrics and convert them into advisory recommendations.

FIELD INSIGHT — How a Confident Advisor Explains a Complex Concept

Clients don't need formulas first — they need clarity first.

Here is a confidence-based communication model you can use immediately:

Concept: *"This property's NOI is $82,000."*

Translation: *"That's the income it keeps after covering its operating expenses — essentially its annual paycheck."*

Strategic meaning: *"A strong NOI makes this asset easier to finance and typically supports a higher valuation."*

Confidence-based delivery: *"So from an investor's perspective, this NOI places the property in a healthy performance range. It gives you stability today and room for strategic growth tomorrow. Let me show you how this compares to similar assets in the submarket."*

This approach does three things simultaneously:

- Simplifies the concept
- Connects the number to the client's priorities
- Positions you as a calm, knowledgeable interpreter of information

Clarity is not a soft skill — it is one of the most profitable skills in multifamily advising.

Communicate Proactively

Expectation principle → proactive clarity prevents uncertainty before it begins.

The number-one complaint clients have about agents is not price, speed, or negotiation — It is silence.

In multifamily real estate, silence is interpreted as uncertainty, and uncertainty weakens trust. Your role is to eliminate ambiguity before it appears.

Clients should never have to ask,

"What's happening with my deal?"

Set expectations early and follow through with precision:

- How often you'll update them
- Which communication channels you'll use
- What the upcoming steps look like

Consistency is the real *"white-glove service."*

FIELD INSIGHT — How Proactive Advisors Eliminate Uncertainty

A well-crafted proactive message might look like this:

***"To keep you fully informed, here's what to expect over the next 48 hours:*

I'll confirm the seller's response window and update you no later than 3 PM tomorrow.

If your offer advances, I'll send a clean summary of timelines: inspection, financing, underwriting.

I'll also share a brief market comparison so you can see how similar properties are performing.

If anything changes sooner, you'll hear from me immediately.

*My goal is for you to always feel one step ahead."***

Clarity reduces anxiety. Structure builds trust.

Proactive communication is leadership.

Empathy Creates Efficiency

Emotional intelligence principle → empathy accelerates decision-making.

It accelerates decision-making by addressing the *real* concern rather than the surface-level objection.

When you understand why a client hesitates — fear, uncertainty, timing, risk tolerance — you no longer waste energy convincing.

You guide.
You clarify.
You remove friction.

Empathy turns hesitation into transparency and transparency into momentum.

A client who feels understood becomes a client who moves confidently.

> FIELD INSIGHT — EMPATHY IN ACTION
>
> A client expresses hesitation about making an offer:
> **Client:** *"I just don't want to make a mistake. What if the numbers don't hold up?"*
>
> **An average agent might push:** *"Inventory is tight — you don't want to miss this opportunity."*
>
> A trusted advisor uses empathy to uncover the real concern.
>
> **Advisor:** *"I completely understand. Let me ask you this — what would you need to feel absolutely confident moving forward?"*
>
> **The client reveals the truth:** *"Honestly… I need to understand the risk if rents dip or expenses rise."*
>
> Now the conversation shifts from emotion → clarity.
> **Advisor:** *"That makes perfect sense. Let's walk through a sensitivity scenario together — what the numbers look like if rents adjust 5%, 8%, or 10%. Once you see that clearly, you'll know exactly where your comfort zone is."*
>
> Empathy turns uncertainty into transparency.
> Transparency turns fear into informed action.

▧ **Cross-Reference:** *For sensitivity analysis, risk scenarios, and stress-testing frameworks, see Chapter 7 — Financial Literacy & Deal Analysis.*

Use Technology to Personalize, Not Automate

Personalization principle → tailored insight builds deeper loyalty.

In Chapter 5, you learned how technology supports prospecting efficiency; here, you'll learn how it elevates the client experience by helping you deliver communication that feels personal, timely, and intentional.

Technology is a tool — not a substitute for presence.

Automation expands your reach, but personalization expands your influence.

World-class advisors don't use technology to distance themselves from their clients; they use it to enhance precision, memory, and meaningful connection.

Your CRM is not a digital address book — it is an intelligence system.

When used intentionally, it becomes the architecture that supports every relationship in your business.

Track details that matter:

- Investment anniversaries
- Preferred communication style
- Property preferences
- Decision-making patterns
- Milestones and personal notes

These details allow you to show up not as a seller — but as a strategic partner.

Technology should help you remember what others forget.

A handwritten note after a tough week, a short-personalized video before a key decision, or a message acknowledging a property anniversary — these touches create long-term loyalty that cannot be automated.

Automation creates efficiency.
Personalization creates longevity.

Master both, and your influence compounds.

Handle Conflict with Grace

Leadership principle → grace in conflict builds long-term trust.

In multifamily real estate, friction is inevitable.

Inspections expose repairs.

Financing hits delays.

Buyers hesitate.

Sellers grow anxious.

Your job is not to eliminate conflict — it is to lead through it.

Clients take emotional cues from your steadiness.

If you remain clear, composed, and structured, their stress reduces immediately.

Start with facts to anchor the moment. Move to feelings to validate the client's experience.

Finish with a next step to restore momentum.

A simple acknowledgment can reset the entire tone of a tense conversation:

"I understand why this is frustrating — let's walk through the next step together."

This one sentence transforms chaos into clarity.

Grace under pressure is not merely professionalism — it is leadership.

Clients remember how you carried them through complexity more than how perfect the transaction was.

Your calm becomes their confidence.

Build a Client Retention System

Legacy principle → retention turns relationships into lifelong value.

A closing is not the end of the relationship — it is the beginning of your long-term influence.

Repetition builds reputation.

Consistency builds familiarity.

Familiarity creates loyalty.

A structured retention system ensures no client ever fades into the background.

Great advisors design intentional touchpoints that deliver value long after the sale.

A world-class retention rhythm looks like:

- 30 days after closing — check-in on the transition
- 6 months — rental performance or valuation update
- 12 months — equity review and strategic planning

These touches shift you from agent to advisor — and advisor to trusted partner.

APPLIED APPLICATION — CLIENT TOUCHPOINT STRATEGY

Create a CRM tag titled **Legacy Clients** and schedule quarterly value-based engagements:

1. **Personalized video check-in**
2. **Property performance snapshot (NOI trend, rent movement, cap-rate shift)**
3. **Local market developments or submarket appreciation insights**
4. **Annual portfolio review invitation — "Let's map out your next step."**

This system turns each client into a long-term asset, each asset into a referral engine, and your name into a trusted brand.

Loyalty is less about the transaction — and more about the relationship you maintain after it.

FIELD INSIGHT — Vanessa's Reputation Revolution

Reliability principle → consistent communication becomes a competitive advantage.

Vanessa wasn't the cheapest or the most experienced agent —
but she became the most trusted.

Her non-negotiable rule was simple:

"Every client gets a response within two hours and a weekly update."

Within six months, her referrals tripled.

Clients remembered her consistency.

They remembered her presence.

They remembered how reliably she showed up — especially during uncertainty.

In a market where most agents communicate reactively, reliability becomes a differentiator.

Consistency is not just professionalism —
it is a revenue stream.

Reflection Point

(Pause and consider before moving forward.)

- How consistent am I in my client communication?
- Do I listen to understand or to respond?
- Where can I add more clarity or empathy?
- Which past clients can I re-engage today with a value-based touchpoint?

Reflection creates alignment.
Alignment strengthens relationships.

▩ LEADERSHIP CHALLENGE — From Communication to Connection

For the next seven days, practice ending **every meaningful conversation** — with a client, colleague, prospect, or partner — with:

"So what I'm hearing is… "

This single reflective phrase strengthens clarity in every interaction.

Watch how it elevates trust, deepens rapport, and improves cooperation — no matter who you're speaking with.

Mastery begins with repetition, not volume.

Key Takeaways

- Trust is built through consistency, not perfection.
- Listening is a competitive advantage.
- Clear explanations accelerate decision-making.
- Empathy shortens the sales cycle.
- Relationships are the real ROI of real estate.

What's Next

You've learned how to build meaningful relationships, elevate communication, and turn trust into your most valuable currency.

In the next chapter, we'll translate that relational mastery into measurable results — analyzing deals with precision, reading performance metrics with confidence, and turning numbers into narratives that drive investor decisions.

Prepare to elevate from conversation to calculation — this is where strategy meets mastery.

"Clients may forget your pitch, but they'll always remember how you made them feel — clear, confident, and valued."

PART III

ADVANCED SKILLS & ANALYTICAL MASTERY

Real mastery begins when instinct and analysis blend into one fluid skill set.

In this part, you move beyond foundational practice into the advanced disciplines that shape professional authority — negotiation, financial clarity, strategic evaluation, and advisory-level insight.

Here, you learn not only how to interpret data, but how to turn it into direction; not only how to manage deals, but how to lead them.

These chapters are designed to refine your judgment, deepen your confidence, and elevate your voice as a multifamily advisor.

This is where technique becomes strategy — and strategy becomes influence.

Chapter 7 — Negotiation Mastery: The Art of Win-Win Deals

Negotiation isn't combat; it's choreography.

Two sides, one rhythm, one goal — movement toward mutual value.

The best negotiators don't dominate; they direct.

Multifamily negotiations carry higher stakes: multiple tenants, larger sums, longer timelines.

To thrive here, you must merge logic with empathy, confidence with composure.

I. Negotiation Begins Long Before the Offer

Preparation is persuasion in disguise.

Most agents think negotiation starts when an offer is written — but the truth is, it starts with your very first conversation.

Every message, showing, and tone of voice sets the emotional stage for how others will respond to you later.

When people feel respected, they become more flexible.

When they feel heard, they become more open.

The most successful negotiators understand this: you're not just negotiating terms — you're negotiating tone.

Every courteous email, every follow-up, every well-timed silence is a rehearsal for agreement.

Think of every phone call as a prelude to the offer — not a transaction, but tone-setting.

Ask about preferred communication style, seller expectations, and decision timelines.

This builds rapport and gives you valuable context long before numbers appear.

When you carry confidence and respect into your first conversations, you lower walls before the real work even begins.

"Win-win happens when everyone feels respected, not defeated."

II. Know Your Numbers

In multifamily sales, value is determined by performance — not presentation.

Properties are evaluated based on how they generate income, how stable that income is, and how sensitive the asset is to operational change.

This is why knowing your numbers matters.

When you understand how income, expenses, and occupancy connect to value, you can explain why a deal works — or why it doesn't — using real outcomes instead of assumptions.

Data is your calm under pressure. Emotion loses power when data enters the room.

Before making or presenting any offer, know:

- Fair-market value and cap-rate averages
- Rent-roll trends and vacancy rates
- Comparable sales and deferred-maintenance costs

Facts create credibility; credibility creates calm.

For instance, if a 12-unit property produces $120,000 annually in NOI and sells for $1.5 million, the cap rate is 8 percent. A vacancy shift of just one unit could reduce NOI by $10,000, lowering the property's value by more than $100,000 — proving how small details drive big decisions.

▧ **Cross-Reference:** *See Chapter 8 — Strategic Deal Analysis: Turning Numbers into Narrative for step-by-step calculations and advanced case studies.*

III. Clarify Your Client's Non-Negotiables

Understanding your client's emotional thresholds is as vital as understanding their financial limits.

When you know what triggers hesitation, you can manage emotion with empathy — not reaction.

Ask early:

"What's one thing you must have — and one condition that would cause you to walk away?"

A clear hierarchy of priorities prevents panic when concessions are needed.

Advisors who can read both numbers and nuance earn trust long before the offer is signed.

IV. Leverage Silence as a Tool

Silence invites information — but it also demonstrates confidence.

A skilled advisor knows that silence is not absence; it's a strategy.

You pause to give others the space to reveal intent, to measure tone, and to regain control of emotional tempo.

When a listing agent or seller goes quiet after receiving your offer, it's not always rejection — it's often reflection.

Behind the silence, decisions are being weighed:

- Is this the strongest offer or just the first?
- How might other parties respond if we delay?
- What leverage do we hold or risk losing?

Silence gives them room to align internally, review contingencies, and strategize before responding.

That quiet space is the negotiation breathing — and it's where leverage takes shape.

➢ ***Keynote*:**

Why Silence Works — Silence creates what psychologists call an *information gap* — a moment where the other party feels compelled to fill the void.

People tend to reveal more when they're slightly uncomfortable, and silence gently nudges them into sharing intentions, priorities, or concessions.

It also activates a subtle power perception: *the person who is most comfortable waiting is perceived as the one in control.*

That's why measured silence strengthens your positioning without a single word spoken.

Guiding Your Client Through the Silence

When representing clients, silence must be paired with reassurance.

After every presentation or offer submission, prepare your client for the natural pause that follows.

Explain that calm waiting often strengthens positioning and perception.

Advisors who master this communication calm tension and reinforce trust.

Knowing When to Follow Up

If silence extends beyond 48 hours on a standard transaction (or 72 for larger commercial deals), a polite, factual check-in is appropriate.

Follow-Up Email Example:

Subject: Following Up — Offer on [Property Address]

Hi [**Agent Name**],

I wanted to check in regarding our recent offer on [**Property Name**]. We remain confident in the opportunity and look forward to learning your seller's feedback.

Please let me know if any additional context or documentation would be helpful.

Best regards,

[**Your Name**]

This maintains professionalism, demonstrates interest without pressure, and keeps communication open.

V. Perception Shapes Power

Perception is the ability to hear what isn't being spoken and see what isn't yet visible.

Skilled negotiators listen beyond words — for hesitation, tone shifts, and timing gaps — translating those cues into calm, confident responses.

Perception creates power because it allows you to adjust positioning before resistance hardens. When you recognize uncertainty, urgency, or flexibility early, you can guide the conversation strategically rather than reacting defensively.

Instead of saying:

"My buyer really wants this deal,"

try:

"My buyer can close quickly and remove uncertainty for your seller."

Reframing transforms pressure into partnership — and perception into power.

VI. Firmness in Motion — Leading with Steady Authority

Not every negotiation remains calm; some require controlled firmness.

Being firm isn't about force — it's about focus.

When clarity must lead, confidence must follow — steady, factual, and without apology.

Firmness earns respect when it is rooted in preparation rather than pressure, and when it holds position without escalating emotion. This distinction becomes clear in practice.

FIELD INSIGHT — ANCHORED CLARITY UNDER PRESSURE

During a negotiation for a 36-unit property, Maya's buyer client hesitated when the seller requested a shorter due-diligence period. The opposing agent pressed hard, saying,

"If your client doesn't agree by today, we have another offer coming in."

Instead of matching that urgency, Maya replied calmly:

"I understand your seller's timeline. My client will respond tomorrow once we've completed our lender's verification."

A solid yes tomorrow is worth more than a rushed maybe today.

Her tone was professional, measured, and unshaken.

By the next afternoon, the seller's agent called back — not only was the deal still on the table, but they accepted Maya's original terms.

Firmness isn't aggression; it's anchored clarity.

It earns respect precisely because it isn't reactionary.

VII. Control Pace, Not People

Tempo is the truth of transaction. Confidence is calm under time pressure.

Never match another person's urgency; guide it.

Rushed decisions feel decisive — but they often sacrifice clarity for speed.

Use checkpoints:

- Clarify → Confirm → Close

Each stage requires understanding before agreement.

The best negotiators conduct tempo, not temperament.

Controlling pace means sensing when to slow dialogue to deepen understanding — and when to accelerate to maintain momentum. Pace is leadership in motion — you're not controlling people; you're directing rhythm.

In practice, professional pace control shows up in three disciplined behaviors:

1. **Slow the Conversation When Stakes Rise**
   Experienced advisors decelerate when tension increases. Clarifying questions reduce emotional velocity and restore alignment:
   "Before we move forward, can we revisit the seller's timeline to ensure we're aligned?"
2. **Hold the Line When Pressure Increases**
   Urgency from the other side never rewrites a client's boundaries. Calm repetition of verified facts preserves authority without confrontation.
3. **Accelerate Only When Certainty Is High**
   Speed becomes an asset after clarity — not before it. Once expectations, terms, and risks are fully understood, momentum turns strategic rather than reactive.

This is how pace becomes leverage — not through force, but through disciplined control of timing, tone, and transition.

APPLIED APLICATION — THE PACE RESET

Agent: *"I understand you'd like to finalize today, but before we rush, let's review the lender's conditions to ensure your position stays strong."*

Client: *"I just don't want to lose the deal."*

Agent: "*You won't — but let's make sure we win the right way. A confident 'yes' tomorrow will always outperform a pressured 'maybe' today.*"

This demonstrates leadership under urgency.

You slow momentum without losing authority — guiding the deal, not chasing it.

VIII. Seek Understanding Before Victory

You can't persuade someone you don't understand.

In negotiation, pushing for agreement before understanding often strengthens resistance.

When an advisor takes the time to uncover what truly matters to the other party, hidden constraints surface — and so do viable paths forward.

Effective negotiators lead with curiosity before conclusion.

Ask open-ended questions:

- *"Help me understand your seller's ideal outcome."*
- *"What would make this a win for both parties?"*

Understanding priorities allows you to shape terms that address real concerns, reduce friction, and keep momentum intact.

Information equals influence.

IX. Close with Confidence and Care

At the end of any negotiation, summarize agreements in writing immediately.

Follow with gratitude:

"It has been an honor and a privilege to serve and collaborate with you on this transaction.

Your professionalism and patience made for a seamless process.

I look forward to working together again."

Gratitude does more than signal politeness — it reinforces mutual respect and strengthens professional rapport.

When parties feel acknowledged, negotiations resolve not as endings, but as continuations of trust.

This closing posture reframes the interaction from a completed transaction into an ongoing relationship, increasing the likelihood of referrals, repeat business, and smoother future negotiations.

Gracious closure is the bridge between deals and long-term partnerships. rhythm within yourself.

Reflection Point

(Pause and consider before moving forward.)

1. How do I prepare emotionally before each negotiation?
2. Do I lead with curiosity or confrontation?
3. Where can I improve clarity when presenting offers?
4. What pattern repeats when negotiations fail — and why?

▩ LEADERSHIP CHALLENGE — FROM OBSERVATION TO ORCHESTRATION

For the next week, study every interaction — not just in deals, but in daily life.

Notice when conversations speed up or stall.

Who leads the tempo? Who follows?

Then, practice adjusting your own rhythm: slow down when others rush, and clarify when others hesitate.

If you're not yet negotiating with clients, apply this exercise in team meetings, calls, or even everyday discussions.

Mastery begins with awareness — not of others' emotions, but of your own pacing power.

You can't lead the rhythm of a deal until you've learned to conduct the rhythm within yourself.

Key Takeaways

- Negotiation is communication, not confrontation.
- Data removes drama; preparation removes panic.
- Listening creates leverage.
- Collaboration compounds credibilit

What's Next

In the next chapter, once a deal merits deeper evaluation, you'll move from negotiation mastery into analytical leadership — learning how to evaluate multifamily opportunities with greater precision, interpret financial data with confidence, and translate numbers into strategic guidance for investors.

This shift from persuasion to evaluation deepens your authority, positioning you not just as a negotiator, but as a trusted advisor capable of guiding decisions that shape long-term value.

Chapter 8 — Financial Literacy for Agents and Investors

Money is the language of real estate.

If you can't read it, you can't negotiate it; if you can't explain it, you can't earn trust.

Financial literacy isn't optional for a multifamily professional — it's the foundation of credibility.

I. You Can't Grow What You Don't Understand

Growth follows understanding.

Without a clear grasp of how value is created, measured, and protected, progress stalls — no matter how strong the effort.

Most agents know how to calculate commission, but not cash flow.
Yet the investor's world runs on math, not marketing.

When you understand how money moves — interest, leverage, taxation, equity — your role changes.

You stop reacting to numbers and start interpreting them.

That shift moves you from salesperson to strategist.

"Confidence in numbers creates confidence in negotiations."

II. Master the Core Formulas

Clarity in numbers builds clarity in decisions.

Every investor conversation you'll ever have rests on seven pillars of financial literacy — screening, income, yield, leverage, safety, and resilience.

Each metric you use sits within one of these pillars and serves a specific purpose in evaluating a property's performance.

Together, they form an interconnected decision framework — where each number feeds the next, shaping valuation, risk, and return.

When agents understand these six pillars, they don't just calculate numbers — they interpret the behavior of a property, speak the language of investors, and elevate their role from salesperson to strategic advisor.

Metric	Formula	Purpose in Practice
GRM (Gross Rent Mulitplier)	Property Price ÷ Gross Annual Rent	Entry-level income screening tool
EGI (Effective Gross Income)	Gross Potential Rent – Vacancy & Credit Loss	Adjusts potential income to reality
NOI (Net Operating Income)	Gross Income – Operating Expenses	Measures operating performance
Cap Rate	NOI ÷ Purchase Price	Value-based return indicator
DSCR (Debt Service Coverage Ratio)	NOI ÷ Debt Payments	Defines lender risk threshold
Cash-on-Cash Return	Annual Pre-Tax Cash Flow ÷ Total Cash Invested	Investor's actual cash yeild
Break-Even Occupancy	(Operating Expenses + Debt Service) ÷ Gross Income	Resilience floor

➢ *Keynote:*

How the Metrics Work Together — Each number feeds the next.

GRM identifies opportunity; **EGI** validates reality; **NOI** measures performance; **Cap Rate** defines market value; **DSCR** governs lending; and lending shapes **Cash-on-Cash Return.**

Understanding this chain transforms basic arithmetic into strategic analysis — giving you control over the financial narrative of every deal.

CONCEPTUAL OVERVIEW — GROSS RENT MULTIPLIER (GRM)

The GRM is a valuation shortcut used to estimate a property's potential return based purely on gross rental income.

It provides a fast, surface-level way to compare properties based solely on income potential — before considering expenses, financing, or tax implications.

It's the entry point of financial analysis, allowing agents and investors to quickly screen deals and identify which assets warrant deeper review.

Formula: GRM = Property Price ÷ Gross Annual Rent

Purpose: The GRM offers a first-glance metric of income efficiency — showing how many years gross rent would take to pay off the purchase price. It's useful for quick comparisons but must always be paired with Cap Rate and NOI for accuracy.

Example: $1,200,000 ÷ $180,000 = 6.7 GRM

Interpretation: A lower GRM suggests stronger gross return. However, two properties may share the same GRM yet differ greatly in expenses — only NOI reveals the truth.

"GRM is your first glance, not your final grade."

➢ ***Keynote:***

Turning Formulas into Fluent Dialogue — Think of formulas as translation tools, not math problems.

When you can say: *"This property's NOI of $90,000 on a $1.2 M purchase yields a 7.5 % cap rate.*
With a 1.35 DSCR, the income easily supports the debt." — you're no longer talking numbers; you're communicating confidence.

APPLIED INSIGHT — Real-World Financial Snapshot (Agent Worksheet Example)

"At an 8 % cap rate and a DSCR of 1.67, this property reflects low-risk cash-flow stability with room for appreciation.

With effective gross income of $180,000 translating to $120,000 in NOI, your break-even occupancy is only 73 % — meaning you can afford three vacant units and still remain profitable.
A strong, data-driven risk-return profile."

Scenario: You're analyzing a 12-unit multifamily property listed at $1,500,000.

Gross Income $180,000 • Operating Expenses $60,000 • Annual Debt Payments $72,000.

The following snapshot translates this interpretation into measurable performance

Metric	Formula	Calculation	Result	Interpretation (What It Means for the Client)
NOI	Gross Income – Operating Expenses	180,000 – 60,000	120,000	True income engine before debt.
Cap Rate	NOI ÷ Purchase Price	120,000 ÷ 1,500,000	8 %	Mid-market return; healthy for risk profile.
Cash-on-Cash Return	(NOI – Debt Service) ÷ Invested Cash	(120,000 – 72,000) ÷ 400,000	12 %	Attractive yield on capital invested.
DSCR	NOI ÷ Debt Payments	120,000 ÷ 72,000	1.67	Lender comfort zone; secure financing.
Break-Even Occ	Expenses + Debt) ÷ Gross Income	(60,000 + 72,000) ÷ 180,000	73 %	Can withstand 27 % vacancy and remain profitable.
GRM	Price ÷ Gross Annual Rent	1,500,000 ÷ 180,000	8.33	Fast screen of income efficiency; needs NOI confirmation.

✍ **Practice Excersise — Build Your Own Snapshot**

Recreate this worksheet using a local listing from your MLS or LoopNet.

Replace each number with real data and write out your interpretations.

Do this once per week to build instinctive financial fluency — the kind investors recognize instantly.

Why it Matters:

Numbers don't replace intuition — they refine it.

When you see formulas as feedback loops rather than calculations, you begin thinking like a portfolio strategist instead of a salesperson.

In that mindset shift lies true financial mastery.

III. Interpreting the Rent Roll

A rent roll is the property's financial DNA — a snapshot of who pays, how much, and for how long.

Here, you learn to read the story behind the income stream — leases, renewals, and risk exposure — not just totals.

Beyond rows of names and numbers, rent rolls reveal the stability, rhythm, and reliability of income — the heartbeat of a multifamily asset.

When you can interpret a rent roll accurately, you don't just assess income; you assess suitability.

You begin identifying which properties can responsibly support a client's goals — and which introduce hidden volatility that should never reach the table.

This level of insight allows you to protect your client, sharpen your deal selection, and anchor recommendations in evidence rather than assumption.

Numbers become narrative.

APPLIED INSIGHT — FROM DATA TO DIAGNOSIS

A rent roll answers four essential questions:

1. Is income consistent? (Rent collection trends)
2. Is growth sustainable? (Renewal and rent escalation trends)
3. Is risk concentrated? (Tenant dependency or lease overlap)
4. Is timing managed? (Lease expirations and turnover pacing)

"Every rent roll tells a story: some whisper stability, others warn of risk."

Core Elements to Examine

Category	What to Review	Why it Matters
Lease Terms	Start and end dates, renewal options	Identifies timing gaps that can cause sudden income loss.
Tenant Mix	Variety of unit types, payment sources	Prevents income reliance on a single demographic or payer.
Rent Escalations	Scheduled increases vs. market rent	Reveals revenue growth potential or under-market exposure.
Payment History	Late payments, NSF occurrences	Indicates operational discipline or management weakness.
Vacancy Timing	Upcoming expirations or clusters	Forecasts turnover periods and staffing needs.
Economic Occupancy	Actual income collected ÷ Scheduled income	Shows how efficiently physical occupancy converts into real revenue — a key indicator of operational performance.

CONCEPTUAL OVERVIEW — Renewal, Delinquency, and Occupancy Stability

The strength of a rent roll lies not in how much rent is collected, but how predictably it's collected.

› Renewal Rate — Stability Indicator

Formula:

Renewal Rate = Renewed Leases ÷ Total Expiring Leases

A healthy multifamily property should maintain renewal rates above **60–70%**.

High renewals signal satisfied tenants and operational efficiency; low renewals hint at pricing issues or service dissatisfaction.

› Delinquency Rate — Reliability Indicator

Formula:

Delinquency Rate = (Delinquent Rent ÷ Scheduled Rent) × 100

A delinquency rate under **3%** indicates stable cash flow.

Anything above **5%** demands scrutiny — chronic late payers erode NOI and lender confidence.

➤ Occupancy Stability — Resilience Indicator

Formula:

Occupancy Rate = (Occupied Units ÷ Total Units) × 100

Consistent occupancy above 90% with low delinquency suggests long-term cash flow reliability.

APPLIED ANALYSIS — Rent Roll Interpretation in Action

Scenario:

You're reviewing a 24-unit rent roll for a buyer client.

The property reports 95% occupancy but reveals this pattern:

Unit Type	Units	Avg Rent	Renewal Rate	Delinquency Rate	Lease Exp Cluster
1-Bed	12	$1,050	83%	2%	4 units expiring May
2-Bed	8	$1,350	60%	6%	5 units expiring June
3-Bed	4	$1,800	50%	0%	All renew July

Interpretation:

The 1-Beds are stable and well-managed — they'll anchor short-term cash flow.

The 2-Beds pose risk: low renewals and high delinquency indicate pricing or maintenance issues.

The 3-Beds show perfect payment history but renewal clustering — signaling potential turnover costs midyear.

Your role as an advisor:

- Flag these for negotiation leverage.
- Recommend the buyer request updated renewal notices before closing.
- Propose a **lease staggering plan** post-acquisition to balance expirations across quarters.

APPLIED APPLICATION — Designing a Lease Staggering Plan

Scenario:

Following your rent-roll review, you discover 10 leases expiring in June — a clear turnover risk

You propose a lease staggering plan to distribute renewals across the year for balanced income flow.

Month	Leases Renewing	Strategy
March	2	Offer early-renewal incentives (2% discount for advance signers).
May	3	Align with spring market demand for easier re-leasing.
July	3	Extend renewals to 14–15 months to shift future expirations out of high-turnover season.
Sept	2	Offer flexible terms to maintain occupancy continuity.

Lease staggering isn't just scheduling — it's stress reduction for property managers and investors alike.

"Even spacing creates predictability. Predictability protects cash flow."

Visualization — Rent Roll Health Grid

Indicator	Healthy Range	Meaning
Renewal Rate	≥ 65%	Strong tenant retention, minimal turnover cost.
Delinquency Rate	≤ 3%	Predictable collections and steady NOI.
Economic Occupancy	≥ 90%	Reliable income alignment with physical occupancy.
Lease Expiration Spread	Evenly distributed	Balanced risk — avoids large vacancy periods.

🗒 *Note:* Healthy rent rolls show balance — renewals and expirations staggered like stepping stones, not cliffs.

ADVISOR INSIGHT — Connecting Rent Rolls to Valuation

Rent rolls aren't just operational documents; they drive property value.

If a property has:

High renewal rates: Investors value predictability → stronger valuation and lower cap rates.

High delinquency: Appraisers discount NOI → lower property value.

Clustered expirations: Underwriters increase risk assumptions → tighter lending terms.

Your ability to interpret these patterns sets you apart as more than an agent — it positions you as a financial storyteller translating numbers into narrative.

💼 In Practice — Read Beyond the Rows

"A rent roll isn't just a record — it's a rhythm."

Numbers tell you what's happening; patterns tell you why."

Learn to listen for the story inside the spreadsheet.

That's where true advisory power begins.

IV. Understand Leverage and Risk

Leverage is the art of control without complete ownership.

In real estate, leverage is what allows ordinary people to control extraordinary assets.

It magnifies opportunity — but it also magnifies error, turning small misjudgments in income, expenses, or timing into outsized consequences

When an advisor understands how leverage behaves under stress, they can distinguish between investments that grow responsibly and those that rely on fragile assumptions.

This insight protects clients from overexposure, guides smarter deal selection, and ensures recommendations are built on durability — not just upside.

The agent or advisor who understands leverage becomes the voice of balance between ambition and prudence.

CONCEPTUAL FOUNDATION — The Double-Edged Sword of Leverage

Leverage is the use of borrowed capital (usually a loan or mortgage) to increase your client's purchasing power — allowing them to control an asset with a smaller amount of their own money.

A $100,000 investment controlling a $1,000,000 asset represents 10:1 leverage.

That same leverage can make you a hero in a rising market — or expose you in a declining one, because leverage multiplies outcomes

When values rise, it amplifies gains; when conditions soften, it magnifies stress.

Leverage itself isn't risky; misunderstanding it is.

To help your clients (and yourself) use it wisely, think of leverage through three filters:

◆ **Return Amplification** — It multiplies both profits and losses.

When leveraged well, a modest increase in property value can create outsized equity gains.

But the same principle applies in reverse — a small dip in rent or market pricing can wipe out years of appreciation overnight.

Advisors who understand this duality coach clients to celebrate returns responsibly and prepare for reversals with equal confidence.

◆ **Liquidity Management** — It demands cash reserves to weather short-term dips.

Leverage magnifies potential, but it also compresses cushion.

The higher the loan-to-value ratio, the thinner the safety net — meaning even brief vacancies or repair costs can cause financial stress.

Healthy investors maintain liquidity equal to at least six months of expenses, ensuring leverage works for them, not against them.

◆ **Psychological Discipline** — It tests patience, especially when markets fluctuate.

Leverage requires more than math; it requires emotional control.

When values dip, inexperienced investors panic-sell, crystallizing losses that might have recovered with time.

Seasoned advisors teach emotional neutrality — to observe, analyze, and adjust, not react — because mindset is the real margin of safety.

CONCEPTUAL FOUNDATION EXPANSION — How to Determine Leverage

Leverage can be viewed two ways — how much control your money buys and how much risk your lender holds.

Leverage Ratio = Total Property Value ÷ Investor's Cash Investment (or inversely, **Loan-to-Value = Loan Amount ÷ Property Value**)

Both tell a story — one about control, the other about risk.

Example 1 — Measuring Control Power (Leverage Ratio)

If an investor puts $200,000 down on a $1,000,000 property:
$1,000,000 ÷ $200,000 = **5:1 leverage**

This means for every $1 of their own money, they control $5 in property value.

Leverage amplifies reach — but the greater the ratio, the greater the volatility.

Here's why:

When you borrow more and own less, even small financial shifts cause larger percentage swings in returns.

For instance:

A $10,000 drop in income may seem small at the property level, but it can materially reduce investor returns—especially when equity is thin

The smaller their personal capital share, the more magnified every dollar of change becomes — in either direction.

This is why seasoned investors say:

"Leverage accelerates success — and magnifies mistakes."

Volatility Visualization — The Leverage Ripple Effect

Investor Equity	Income Drop	Impact on Equity Value
$500,000 (2:1 leverage)	-$10,000	-2% loss
$200,000 (5:1 leverage)	-$10,000	-5% loss
$100,000 (10:1 leverage)	-$10,000	-10% loss

Higher leverage magnifies every shift — profit or pain.

Note: The greater the leverage, the smaller your cushion. The smaller the cushion, the greater the movement.

Example 2 — Measuring Safety Cushion (Loan-to-Value, LTV)

$800,000 (loan) ÷ $1,000,000 (value) = 80% LTV

From a lender's perspective:

Higher LTV = higher perceived risk (less borrower equity).

Lower LTV = greater borrower stability (more personal stake).

Most lenders prefer ≤ 75% LTV to allow for borrower accountability and property resilience.

In Practice — Two Views, One Truth

The Investor's View: *"How much value can I control?"*

The Lender's View: *"How much risk can I absorb?"*

Your mastery lies in translating between the two.

Stability is not about eliminating leverage — it's about engineering tolerance for turbulence.

APPLIED APPLICATION — THE $1M LEVERAGE COMPARISON

Investor	Down PYMT	Loan AMT	NOI	Annual Debt Service	Cash Flow	Result
Investor A **(Conservative)**	$300,000 (70% LTV)	$700,000	$90,000	$60,000	$30,000	10% CoC
Investor A **(Aggresive)**	$150,000 (85% LTV)	$850,000	$90,000	$75,000	$15,000	10% CoC

At first glance, both earn similar returns — until something changes.

If vacancy increases by just **10%**, NOI drops to **$81,000**:

- Investor A still earns **$21,000**
- Investor B breaks even

This is the silent cost of over-leverage — small shifts erase stability.

Interpreting the Ratios — What to Watch For

Metric	Ideal Range	Meaning
Loan-to-Value (LTV)	≤ 75%	Maintains equity cushion to absorb fluctuations.
DSCR	≥ 1.25	Ensures income comfortably covers debt.
Reserve Coverage	6 months expenses	Protects against unexpected vacancies or repairs.

▸ *Keynote:*

When advising clients:

- Stress-test deals — simulate a 10% drop in rent or a rise in interest rates.
- Teach clients to view cash reserves as insurance for leverage.
- Remind them: **equity grows slowly, but stability compounds faster.**

CONCEPTUAL FOUNDATION — The Dynamic Trinity of Cash Flow

› NOI = Performance Pulse

The measure of operational efficiency — what's earned after expenses but before debt.

When NOI rises sustainably, every other metric strengthens.

› **DSCR = Safety Margin**

The lender's comfort zone.

DSCR tells you how much cushion exists between income and debt.

A **DSCR** of 1.25 means income exceeds loan payments by 25%.

Below 1.0, the property's income no longer covers its debt — a flashing red light.

› **Cash-on-Cash Return = Investor Reward**

This ratio converts the performance and safety above into what the investor actually feels — their personal yield.

Strong **NOI** and **DSCR** protect the investor's principal; Cash-on-Cash defines their satisfaction.

*"The moment you understand how **NOI** fuels **DSCR**, and how **DSCR** protects **Cash-on-Cash**, you stop seeing metrics as numbers — and start seeing them as cause and effect."*

CONCEPTUAL FOUNDATION EXPANSION — Forecasting Deal Resilience

Resilience analysis connects these three metrics over time, showing how a property behaves under variable conditions.

Advisors who can model these relationships become trusted strategists.

Scenario 1 — Stable Market

• NOI = $120,000 Debt Service = $80,000

→ **DSCR = 1.50 Cash-on-Cash = 10%**

☑ Healthy margin; lender and investor aligned.

Scenario 2 — Moderate Vacancy (10% Drop in Income)

• NOI = $108,000 Debt Service = $80,000

→ **DSCR = 1.35 Cash-on-Cash** = 7.5%

⚠ Cushion remains, but investor yield begins to compress.

Scenario 3 — Market Correction (20% Drop in Income)

• NOI = $96,000 Debt Service = $80,000

→**DSCR = 1.20 Cash-on-Cash = 5%**

❗ Approaching lender watchlist territory; liquidity reserves become critical.

📝 Note: Your DSCR measures the deal's heartbeat; your Cash-on-Cash measures its endurance. When the heartbeat weakens but the endurance collapses, the property isn't just stressed — it's signaling the need for intervention.

Visualization — The Cash Flow Continuum

Market Condition	NOI	DSCR	Cash-onCash Return	Investor Health Signal
Expansion (+10% NOI)	$132,000	1.65	12%	Growth Phase —room to leverage or invest
Normal	$120,000	1.50	10%	Balanced Performance
Moderate Vacancy (-10%)	$108,000	1.35	7.5%	Monitor Cash Flow
Correction (-20%)	$96,000	1.20	5%	Trigger Liquidity Plan
Stress Test (-30%)	$84,000	1.05	2%	At Risk —requires capital support

"The continuum reveals a truth many overlook: cash flow rarely fails suddenly — it fades gradually, and each fade has a meaning."

APPLIED APPLICATION — STRESS-TESTING FOR CONFIDENCE

When reviewing or presenting deals, run three cash-flow scenarios:

- **Base Case:** Expected NOI
- **Optimistic Case:** +10% NOI growth
- **Conservative Case:** –10% to –20% NOI decline

This gives clients an emotional map of what could happen — best, typical, and worst.

Show them how long reserves or rent growth can sustain debt coverage at each level.

📋 ***Note:*** *"The best negotiators aren't surprised by downturns — they've already priced them in."*

APPLIED INSIGHT — Connecting Metrics to Meaning

When explaining cash-flow performance:

• **If NOI improves but DSCR remains flat** → debt terms may be absorbing gains.

• **If Cash-on-Cash rises faster than NOI** → equity efficiency is improving.

• **If DSCR falls faster than NOI** → debt load is outpacing income.

Reading these relationships helps you advise confidently during acquisition, refinancing, or disposition discussions.

"Data describes a deal. Interpretation defines its destiny."

💼 **In Practice — Forecasting as Leadership**

"To forecast cash flow is to forecast confidence.
When you can model tomorrow's numbers today, clients stop seeing you as a salesperson — they see you as their financial compass."

Numbers Are Narrative

Numbers tell stories — but only to those fluent enough to listen.

Behind every ratio is a rhythm; behind every formula, a forecast.

Financial literacy isn't about memorizing calculations — it's about recognizing patterns of possibility and patterns of risk.

When you can interpret **GRM** as opportunity, **NOI** as operational health, **DSCR** as financial resilience, and Cash-On-Cash return as sustainability —

you're no longer reading a spreadsheet; you're evaluating whether a strategy can responsibly support a client's goals.

This level of fluency allows advisors to distinguish between deals that look impressive on paper and those that perform reliably over time.

True mastery isn't just knowing the math — it's knowing what the math is signaling before a recommendation is made.

Because in multifamily real estate, numbers don't lie — they lead.

Reflection Point

(Pause and consider before moving forward.)

As you move deeper into financial analysis, consider where your confidence truly comes from.

Are you relying on formulas to tell you what a deal is worth, or are you developing the judgment to interpret what the numbers are revealing?

The difference between calculation and analysis is not technical skill — it is clarity of thought.

An effective multifamily advisor understands not just how to compute value, but how to question assumptions, recognize risk signals, and explain financial outcomes with confidence and restraint.

▩ LEADERSHIP CHALLENGE — Financial Fluency in Action

For the next seven days, review one real property per day.

Calculate its NOI, Cap Rate, and Cash-on-Cash Return.

Then write one sentence that translates those numbers into meaning for a client or investor.

By week's end, you'll no longer see data — you'll see decisions.

What's Next

In this chapter, you learned to translate financial data into strategic insight.

You discovered how GRM reveals opportunity, how NOI measures performance, how DSCR protects stability, and how leverage shapes both growth and risk.

You learned that cash flow isn't just math — it's movement, revealing whether a deal breathes with strength or strain.

You now speak the language of financial literacy:
You can analyze, interpret, and explain — not just calculate.

That fluency is what turns confidence into credibility and transforms agents into trusted advisors.

In the next chapter, you'll take that fluency further — applying it to your own enterprise.

You'll learn how to structure profits, budgets, and reserves with the same precision you bring to property analysis,
building not just portfolios for clients — but wealth strategies for yourself.

Chapter 9 — Strategic Deal Analysis for Agents and Investors

Where financial literacy becomes financial leadership.

You've learned the language of numbers.
Now you'll learn how to make those numbers speak for your client.

Strategic deal analysis transforms raw data into insight, insight into confidence, and confidence into decisive action. In the multifamily world, every seasoned investor and trusted agent understands one truth: numbers tell the story long before opinions ever can.

Deal analysis isn't about spreadsheets — it's about understanding behavior through numbers. When you interpret numbers accurately, you reveal how a property breathes: its stability, its sensitivity, and its long-term strength.

Neutral interpretation gives you power: it earns respect, builds trust, and anchors your reputation as a professional who leads with logic, not impulse.

Even if you're not representing institutional investors, understanding these principles positions you as a higher-caliber professional. It allows you to explain value, qualify opportunities, and speak the language of investment — skills that distinguish multifamily advisors from generalist agents.

When you master analysis, you don't chase deals — you shape them.

Let's begin.

I. Strategic Deal Analysis — The Role of Numbers in Advisory Leadership

Where numbers become screening criteria, not just calculation

In strategic deal analysis, numbers serve a role far beyond calculation.

They function as filters, signals, and decision guides — shaping how opportunities are evaluated, risks are identified, and recommendations are formed.

Rather than being used to justify decisions after the fact, numbers guide judgment in real time.

They help advisors screen opportunities efficiently, recognize patterns that narrative alone can obscure, and lead investors with clarity and confidence.

Numbers — How They Function at the Advisory Level

- Filter opportunity — quickly distinguishing viable deals from distractions before time and resources are wasted.
- Reveal risk — exposing weaknesses in income stability, expense assumptions, and capital structure.
- Support judgment — grounding recommendations in data while allowing experience and context to guide interpretation.
- Translate complexity into confidence — helping investors understand not just what the numbers say, but what they mean for performance and long-term value.

This may appear when an advisor reviews two properties with similar projected returns, yet recognizing that one carries hidden renewal risk and expense instability not reflected in the pro forma.

💼 **In Practice — Using Numbers to Lead Decisions**

An effective advisor doesn't simply report metrics; they interpret what those metrics reveal about stability, risk, and long-term performance.

In practice — this means looking beyond surface projections to question assumptions, identify pressure points, and prioritize opportunities that align with an investor's objectives.

Rather than reacting to attractive figures, use numbers to frame the conversation, shape expectations, and lead clients toward informed, disciplined decisions.

II. Start with the Right Data — Verification Before Interpretation

Garbage in = garbage out.

Every great analysis begins with truth — and truth starts with clean, verified data.

No amount of modeling can fix what begins in error. A single inflated rent figure or missing expense line can distort your valuation and derail your credibility.

The accuracy of your conclusions depends on the accuracy of your sources.

As a rule, never calculate from assumption. Calculate from verification

Before you model, verify.
Before you calculate, confirm.

APPLIED APPLICATION — The Intake Checklist (One-Minute Gate)

Before you begin modeling, run this one-minute audit of your inputs:

Your essential data set should include:

- Purchase price and financing terms (rate, amortization — the scheduled repayment period of the loan principal — loan-to-value, and prepayment details).
- Current rent roll and occupancy history (physical and economic occupancy, not pro forma projections — "pro forma" refers to projected future income or expenses that haven't yet occurred, useful for forecasting but unreliable for initial analysis until verified).
- Operating expenses (utilities, management, insurance, maintenance, taxes, reserves).
- Trailing-12 (T-12) income and expense statement (to identify seasonal or cyclical performance trends).
- Market rents and comparable sales (for pricing, yield, and value benchmarking).
- Debt quote or lender term sheet (to confirm DSCR, leverage, and reserve requirements).
- Property condition summary or inspection notes (to link physical health to financial durability).

If any one of these is missing or incomplete, pause the analysis and request them.

Why it Matters:

Incomplete data leads to inaccurate conclusions — and inaccuracy costs trust.

When you insist on verified, current inputs, you safeguard your client's capital and your own credibility.

In a market full of assumptions, the agent who works from evidence becomes the advisor investors call first — and last.

Discipline in data builds confidence in counsel — and confidence is the currency of leadership in real estate.

III. The Quick Scan — Rapid Deal-Worthiness Test

Efficiency saves energy.

Before diving into a spreadsheet, determine if a deal is even worth your time.

Ask three essential questions:

- Does the property meet minimum return thresholds?
- Is it in a stable or improving submarket?
- Does its physical condition align with its asking price?

This step determines whether a deal warrants deeper analysis or should be ruled out early.

A sharp real estate advisor knows that the first look often reveals whether the deal is worth the next hour of modeling.

APPLIED APPLICATION — The "First Glance" Filter in Action

You receive two listings in the same submarket:

Property A:

24 units, listed at $3.6M, advertised as an "8% cap rate."

No rent roll, no trailing-T-12 expenses, and four units "under renovation."

You pause — these gaps mean you'd be analyzing guesses, not data.

📝 Note: "Insufficient data — hold until verified."

Property B:

20 units, listed at $3.2M, 96% occupied, with a full rent roll, tax statement, and T-12 provided.

Market comps show similar properties at 7.8% cap rates, trending upward.

📝 Note: "Complete data package — proceed to deeper analysis."

That's the value of the Quick Scan — it protects your time and your judgment.

Discipline is the first line of profitability.

The 90-Second Rule

If two of three pillars (**location, income, condition**) fail your analysis standard, don't model yet.

Clarify. Correct. Or cut.

Every minute you spend on the wrong deal delays the right one.

Clients notice the professional who says,

"Let's pause this review until we have complete data — here's what we still need."

When you master the art of early elimination, you replace busywork with strategy — and strategy builds wealth.

That restraint reads as integrity, not hesitation.

That's how efficiency becomes excellence.

📓 **Cross-Reference:** *See Chapter 8 – Master the Core Formulas* (sections on *GRM, DSCR, and Break-Even Occupancy).*

IV. Calculating Core Metrics — Let the Math Speak First

Once you've gathered verified data and passed your Quick Scan, it's time to translate reality into numbers.

Numbers bring objectivity — they anchor every conversation in truth rather than opinion.

Core metrics serve as the blueprint for valuation and risk analysis:

- **NOI (Net Operating Income)** — Gross Income minus Operating Expenses.
- **Cap Rate** — NOI ÷ Purchase Price.
- **Cash-on-Cash Return** — Annual Pre-Tax Cash Flow ÷ Total Cash Invested.
- **Break-Even Occupancy** — (Operating Expenses + Debt Service) ÷ Gross Income.
- **IRR (Internal Rate of Return)** — Measures long-term profitability across the holding period.

Each formula is a window into performance, risk, and opportunity.

Use these to benchmark performance against comparable properties.

APPLIED APPLICATION — "Two-Layer Math"

Every deal has two realities — *what it is today* and *what it can become.*

Layer 1 — Today

Analyze current rents and expenses only.

This represents the property as it truly performs — not as it promises.

Example:

If the rent roll shows $1,000 per unit with consistent 95% occupancy, your baseline income isn't hypothetical — it's proven.

You're establishing a factual foundation before forecasting potential.

Layer 2 — Stabilized

Model verified improvements: document what changes, when, and why.

Only include adjustments that can be executed and evidenced (e.g., signed lease renewals, confirmed rent increases, approved expense reductions).

Example:

If two leases renew next month at $1,150 and you've verified comparable rents at that rate, that's a legitimate improvement — not speculation.

Present both layers side-by-side to show reality *and* potential — without inflating either.

Your clients will learn to trust your precision more than your pitch.

> 💼 **In Practice — Applied Layered Analysis**
>
> You're analyzing a 10-unit property listed for $1,200,000.
>
> The seller claims, *"Rents can go up 20% after renovation."*
>
> Instead of guessing, you separate the layers:
>
> **Layer 1 (Current):**
>
> - Average rent = $1,000 × 10 units = $120,000 annual gross
> - Operating expenses = $45,000
>
> ➢ **NOI = $75,000 → Cap Rate = 6.25%**
>
> **Layer 2 (Stabilized):**
>
> - Local comps confirm $1,150/month post-upgrade (+15%, not 20%)
> - Renovation budget = $40,000
> - Revised income = $138,000; expenses constant → NOI = $93,000
>
> ➢ **Cap Rate (after stabilization)** = 7.75%
>
> **Interpretation:**
>
> Layer 1 shows where the property is.
> Layer 2 shows where it can go.
> That difference — documented and defensible — builds credibility.

▧ **Cross-Reference:** See *Chapter 8 — Core Formulas & Advanced Cash Flow Insights* for DSCR interactions, stress testing, and multi-scenario forecasting models.

V. Conduct Sensitivity Analysis — Testing Stress, Not Hope

Test performance, not potential

Sensitivity analysis lets you measure how much stress a property can absorb before performance weakens. By adjusting rent, expense, and financing variables, you visualize resilience instead of relying on optimism.

Every projection hides assumptions: **rent growth, vacancy, interest rates.**

Testing those assumptions converts confidence from emotional to mathematical.

A property isn't strong because it performs well in a spreadsheet — it's strong because it survives when the spreadsheet bends.

Run *"what-if"* scenarios:

- What if rents drop 5 %?
- What if expenses rise 10 %?
- What if interest rates increase 1 %?

Sensitivity analysis helps you prepare clients for reality, not fantasy.

This analysis builds directly on the stress-testing models introduced in Chapter 8. Review those examples to see how cash flow, DSCR, and investor yield interact under changing conditions.

▧ **Cross-Reference:** *See Chapter 8 — Advanced Cash Flow Insights for DSCR and Cash-on-Cash interaction modeling and multi-scenario forecasting.*

APPLIED APPLICATION — Stress-Testing in a Real Deal

You're analyzing a 16-unit property listed at $2,400,000.
Current rents average $1,200 per unit, with 5 % vacancy and $80,000 annual expenses.

Debt service is projected at $120,000 per year.

Base Case — Performance at Stability

- Gross Potential Income = $1,200 × 16 × 12 = $230,400
- Effective Gross Income (95%) = $218,880
- NOI = $218,880 – $80,000 = $138,880
- DSCR = $138,880 ÷ $120,000 = 1.16
- Cash-on-Cash = ($18,880 ÷ $600,000) = 3.1%

The deal appears thin but viable — earning slightly above debt obligations.

Understanding Shifts Step by Step

When markets tighten, one variable change ripples through every metric.

Watch how rent and expense movement transforms NOI and DSCR.

Base Case — Understanding Shifts Step by Step

- Gross Potential Income (GPI) = $230,400
- Vacancy (5%) = $11,520 → EGI = $218,880
- Operating Expenses = $80,000

➢ NOI = $138,880 DSCR = 1.16

Everything operates smoothly — the property earns comfortably above debt obligation

■ Case A — Rent Drop 5 %

- EGI falls 5% → $218,880 × 0.95 = $207,936
- Expenses remain $80,000

➢ NOI = $127,936 DSCR ≈ 1.07 CoC = 1.3%

Margins compress. The property still pays debt, but with little buffer.

■ **Case B — Expense Increase 10 %**

- EGI stable at $218,880
- Expenses rise 10% → $88,000

➢ NOI = $130,880 DSCR ≈ 1.09 CoC = 1.8%

Slightly stronger than a rent decline, but the cushion remains thin.

■ **Case C — Rent Drop 5 % + Expense Increase 10 %**

- EGI = $207,936
- Expenses = $88,000

➢ NOI = $119,936 DSCR ≈ 1.00 (Break-Even) CoC ≈ 0.0%

The property now rides the line — one late rent cycle could push it into negative cash flow.

"Every percentage point tells a story.
Reading its tone is what separates reaction from readiness."

Interpretation:

The property can absorb a small shock but not two at once.

That's your narrative for the client: **"This deal performs only in stability — it's not resilient yet."**

Visualization — Mini Sensitivity Grid

Variable	Base	Case A (-5% Rent)	Case B (+10% Expense)	Case C (Both)
NOI	$138,880	$127,936	$130,880	$119,936
DSCR	1.16	1.07	1.09	1.00
CoC	3.2%	1.3%	1.8%	0.0%

Why it Matters:

Sensitivity analysis builds credibility through clarity.

It turns the vague question — *"Is this a good deal?"* — into a defined answer:

"How far can this deal bend before it breaks?"

When you can show that story with precision, clients see you not just as an agent, but as an analyst who leads with logic.

VI. Precision Builds Persuasion

At this stage, your skill is no longer in running numbers — it's in translating them.

Precision transforms analysis from arithmetic into authority. The more exact your interpretations, the more persuasive your guidance becomes.

When clients see that you can quantify both risk and resilience, your words carry weight beyond opinion — they signal mastery.

In multifamily, that precision is the difference between:

- a guess and a grounded recommendation,
- a nervous decision and a confident one,
- a hopeful investor and a strategic one.

What Precision Actually Does

1. **It neutralizes emotion.**
   When a client is anxious or excited, precise metrics create clarity and stabilize thinking.

2. **It turns numbers into narratives.**
   Clients do not remember formulas; they remember what the numbers *mean.*

3. **It elevates your authority.**
   When you walk into the conversation with thresholds, breakpoints, DSCR clarity, and risk parameters, your presence shifts from salesperson to strategist.

APPLIED APPLICATION — How Precision Sounds in Practice

Instead of:

"This deal looks good. I think cash flow should work."

You say:

"At a 1.32 DSCR and a break-even occupancy of 76%, this property maintains positive cash flow even with a 10% rent decline. That puts it within our risk tolerance and signals operational resilience."

That one sentence tells the client: you've tested the numbers, you understand the thresholds, and you can explain the deal's strength in plain language.

Precision reduces risk by replacing assumption with interpretation.

The more exact your language, the more exact your client's decision-making becomes.

VII. Communication in Practice

Your ability to interpret numbers is your technical skill.

Your ability to *translate* those numbers is your professional power.

Many agents stop at analysis — presenting accurate data and assuming the conclusion is self-evident.

Advisors advance their careers by mastering communication: the ability to frame numbers with context, guide interpretation, and bridge the gap between information and informed decision-making.

Why it Matters:

Numbers overwhelm without context.

- Clients need clarity, not complexity.
- The deal lives or dies on how well the story behind the numbers is told.

CONCEPTUAL OVERVIEW — From Data → Dialogue

Below are paired examples demonstrating how to elevate communication without diluting accuracy.

Without Precision:

"Income is good, so we should be okay on the loan."

With Analytical Clarity:

"At its current NOI, the DSCR is 1.32. That means income exceeds debt obligations by 32%, giving us a safe operating buffer even under mild vacancy pressure."

Without Structure:

"I think rents could go up."

With Evidence:

"Current rents are $1,150. Market-supported rents average $1,275 based on the comps we verified. That creates a documented 10% rent lift — not a speculative one."

Without Interpretation:

"The pro forma shows better numbers."

With Explanation:

"The pro forma assumes $18,000 in reduced expenses, but those reductions remove management and underestimate repairs. When we reinstate realistic operating costs, NOI adjusts to its true baseline."

Clients trust what they understand — and they understand what you make simple.

When you speak in metrics — clearly, calmly, and confidently — your analysis becomes leadership. Your numbers give clients emotional permission to make confident decisions.

▧ **Cross-Reference:** *See Chapter 6 — Communicating Complex Ideas Simply for phrasing strategis that make financial data conversational and client-friendly.*

VIII. Evaluate Upside Potential — Turning Opportunity into Evidence

Potential is profit with a plan.

Every great deal carries unrealized opportunity — but only when that opportunity is identified, verified, and executed with discipline.

Ask three critical questions:

1. Can rents be increased without losing tenants?
2. Can expenses be reduced without cutting quality?
3. Can amenities or management improvements justify higher value?

The best deals are rarely perfect; they're potential waiting to be optimized.

Upside isn't imagination — it's verification.

A professional doesn't "hope" for better numbers; they document the path that creates them.

CONCEPTUAL CLARIFICATION — Market-Verified vs. Assumption-Based Upside

Not all upside is created equal.

Some upside is market-verified — supported by comparable rents, vacancy trends, operational quotes, or documented performance benchmarks.

Other upside is assumption-based — dependent on speculation, aggressive forecasting, or idealized renovation outcomes.

A professional distinguishes between the two immediately.

Market-verified upside strengthens valuation.

Assumption-based upside inflates it.

Advisors must train clients to recognize this difference early, because it protects them from overpaying for performance that does not yet exist.

APPLIED APPLICATION — The Evidence of Upside

You're reviewing a 20-unit building listed for $2.8 million.

Current rents average $1,150, but similar properties in the area average $1,275.

That means this building is renting about 10% below the market, which is a clear opportunity for improvement.

Operating expenses also look inflated because the property is paying a 9% management fee, while the typical fee in this market is closer to 6%.

When you model realistic operational improvements, two things stand out:

1. Rent Growth (supported by comps): +10%

This means the units are simply under-market.

Bringing rents in line with neighborhood averages wouldn't require major renovations — just better management and normal turnover.

For example:

Raising average rent from **$1,150 → $1,275** is a reasonable, achievable increase supported by actual market data — about an 11% increase.

2. Expense Correction (supported by quotes): –3% gross

Reducing the management fee from 9% to 6% brings expenses back in line with the market.

This isn't speculation — it's a correction supported by real, verifiable data.

Resulting NOI Increase: +$34,000 annually

These two improvements raise the property's annual Net Operating Income (**NOI**) by **$34,000.**

Valuation Impact at a 7.25% Cap Rate:
$34,000 ÷ 0.0725 = $469,000

💡 What This Means in Plain Terms

You've created nearly half a million dollars in property value —
not by gambling or "hoping the market goes up,"
but by aligning rents with market reality and correcting an inflated expense.

This is called **forced appreciation**, and it's one of the most powerful wealth-building tools in multifamily real estate.

◆ How to Explain This to a Client:

"Because the rents were about 11% below where the market already supports them, and because expenses were higher than normal, correcting those two issues naturally increases the property's income. In multifamily, income drives value.
So improving operations by even a small amount can create hundreds of thousands of dollars in immediate equity."

◆ **From Analysis to Advisory**

Upside isn't just about identifying opportunity; it's about *communicating it clearly.*

When you can walk a client through how operational improvements translate to tangible value, you transform abstract math into financial vision.

◆ **Feasibility vs. Possibility**

Every deal presents possibilities, but only some present feasible pathways.

Feasibility requires three conditions:

1. **Evidence** that change is achievable (market rents, quotes, comps).
2. **A realistic timeline** for execution.
3. **Operational stability** to support the improvement without destabilizing cash flow.

This distinction is a hallmark of sophisticated analysis.

Professionals do not simply identify what could happen — they evaluate what can happen based on documented reality.

Why it Matters:

This example shows that wealth in multifamily isn't found — it's engineered.

The ability to calculate, interpret, and explain value creation turns you from an agent into a financial strategist.

It proves that mastery isn't about bigger deals — it's about sharper insight.

IX. Forced Appreciation — The Investor's Power Lever

Forced appreciation isn't luck — it's leadership.

It represents one of the most powerful value-creation levers in multifamily real estate — not because the market grants it, but because the investor engineers it.

Unlike market appreciation, which depends on external trends or economic momentum, forced appreciation is rooted in ***control, clarity, and intentional action.***

It is predictable, repeatable, and directly tied to operational excellence.

At its core, forced appreciation emerges when an investor strategically increases a property's income or reduces its expenses in a way that strengthens Net Operating Income **(NOI)** — and therefore, property value.

In multifamily, **income defines value**, which means small shifts in performance can produce large shifts in equity.

Key Drivers of Forced Appreciation

1. Income Growth — Aligning Rents With Market Reality

Rents that lag behind competitive properties create immediate and measurable opportunity.

Income growth may come from:

- Raising rents to current market levels
- Adding new income streams such as parking, storage, pet rent, or premium units
- Improving unit finishes to justify higher rental tiers

When done responsibly — and supported by verifiable market data — income growth becomes one of the cleanest and most defensible paths to value creation.

2. Expense Efficiency — Reducing Waste Without Reducing Quality

Forced appreciation is not cost-cutting for the sake of cutting.

It is the optimization of controllable expenses while maintaining — or improving — the resident experience.

Examples include:

- Renegotiating management fees
- Implementing utility reimbursements or submetering
- Updating maintenance workflows
- Replacing outdated contracts with competitive bids

Each efficiency strengthens NOI without compromising operations.

3. Operational Stabilization — Engineering Predictable Income

Volatility is the enemy of value because income uncertainty increases perceived risk.

When cash flow fluctuates, buyers discount projections, lenders tighten underwriting assumptions, and investors demand higher returns to compensate for instability.

Operational stabilization reduces that risk by making income predictable rather than reactive.

Consistent performance allows decision-makers to model future cash flow with greater confidence, which directly influences pricing, loan terms, and investor appetite.

Stabilization strategies typically focus on:

■ Reducing delinquency to protect reliable monthly income and limit collection risk.

■ Increasing renewal consistency to stabilize turnover costs and forecast occupancy.

■ Staggering lease expirations to prevent concentrated vacancy exposure.

■ Strengthening tenant screening criteria to improve payment reliability and tenure.

■ Improving occupancy management to smooth income patterns over time.

When income behaves consistently, assets become easier to underwrite, easier to finance, and easier to value.

Operational stability signals control — and control is rewarded in valuation through stronger pricing, tighter cap rates, and more favorable lending terms.

CONCEPTUAL CONNECTION — Why It Works

When income rises and expenses fall, NOI increases — and in multifamily, income defines value.

Unlike residential real estate — which is valued based on comparable sales — multifamily assets are valued primarily based on their income stream.

Even modest operational improvements can create exponential equity growth, because valuation is tied directly to NOI through the cap rate.

Example:

A $10,000 increase in annual NOI at a 7 % cap rate =
$10,000 ÷ 0.07 = $142,857 in added property value.

▸ ***Keynote:***

Forced appreciation is the art of earning equity faster than the market can deliver it.

It rewards:

- Skill
- Strategy
- Execution
- Precision

Agents who can identify and communicate forced appreciation opportunities elevate themselves from transaction facilitators to trusted investment advisors.

They become the professionals who don't wait for value — **they reveal it.**

Your job is not only to quantify opportunity but to articulate it clearly:

"When we increase income or reduce inefficiencies in a way the market supports, we're not hoping for better performance — we're engineering it. And in multifamily, engineered performance creates immediate equity."

This transforms abstract math into strategic clarity for your client.

💼 In Practice — Create Value, Don't Wait for It

Market appreciation rewards patience.

Forced appreciation rewards performance.

That's why seasoned advisors don't wait for value — they help their clients create it.

Every time you identify an inefficiency, restructure management, or reveal unrealized income, you're not just analyzing — you're engineering equity.

That's what separates the average agent from the multifamily strategist.

You're not just analyzing numbers —
you're engineering outcomes.

X. Factor in Financing — Understanding How Financing Shapes Return, Risk, and Client Strategy

Financing can make or break a deal — not just for the investor, but for the agent guiding them.

The structure of the loan directly influences cash flow, equity growth, and overall return.

A strong agent understands how to analyze and explain these differences clearly to their clients.

Professional Note: **While I am not a lender and do not convey any knowledge as if I were one, the information in this section is provided strictly for educational and informational purposes. Agents should always encourage their clients to consult with a licensed mortgage lender or financial advisor for personalized financing guidance and loan qualification details.**

APPLIED APPLICATION — COMPARE LOAN STRUCTURES

Fixed-Rate Loans

Provide predictable payments and long-term stability. They often carry slightly higher rates, but they insulate the buyer from market volatility — meaning the monthly payment remains constant even if interest rates rise.

Risk-averse clients are those who prioritize stability and peace of mind over maximizing short-term returns. They prefer knowing exactly what their payment will be each month, allowing them to plan confidently and avoid surprises.

Long-hold strategies refer to investors who intend to keep the property for an extended period — typically seven to ten years or more. These clients focus on gradual appreciation, consistent cash flow, and building equity over time rather than flipping for quick profit.

For these clients, a fixed-rate loan becomes a powerful tool: it locks in cost certainty, aligns with their timeline, and protects consistency — a key selling point during uncertain rate cycles.

Adjustable-Rate Loans (ARMs)

Offer lower initial rates and can improve short-term cash flow, but carry exposure to future rate increases.

Agents must help clients evaluate when the initial savings justify the potential risk, especially if the hold period is shorter than the adjustment window.

➢ *Keynote:*

For clients who plan to reposition or sell within a few years, an **ARM** can create early flexibility. However, for those uncertain of their exit plan, rate adjustments can disrupt cash flow and erode projected returns.

Bridge Loans

Short-term, flexible financing tools often used for value-add or repositioning projects.

They come with higher interest rates but allow buyers to close quickly and execute renovations or operational improvements before refinancing into permanent debt.

Bridge financing is ideal for clients executing forced appreciation strategies — when used with a clear, time-bound exit plan.

Example:

An investor purchases a 20-unit building with below-market rents. By using a 12-month bridge loan, they can modernize units, raise rents to market levels, and refinance into a long-term fixed loan at a higher valuation — effectively creating equity through performance.

Key Metrics to Understand

Amortization Schedule — Based on the finalized loan terms

Shows how each payment divides between interest and principal over time. A 30-year term keeps payments lower and improves cash flow, while a 20-year term builds equity faster but increases monthly cost.

Example:

If a client buys a $1 million property at 6% interest:
• On a 30-year schedule, payments are lower — more liquidity now.

• On a 20-year schedule, payments are higher — but principal reduction happens faster, allowing the owner to build equity and increase net worth more rapidly over time.

How to Convey This to Your Client Confidently:

You might say —

"The amortization schedule tells us how your loan balance shrinks over time. With a 30-year term, your payments stay comfortable and free up more monthly cash flow, but equity builds slower. With a 20-year term, you're paying down the principal faster — meaning you own more of your property sooner and create long-term wealth through equity growth."

Deliver it in plain, conversational language — like you're showing them their future.

Clients don't remember formulas; they remember the feeling of progress and ownership.

When you can paint that picture, you turn numbers into trust.

Prepayment Penalties

Certain loans charge a fee if the borrower refinances or pays off early.

These clauses protect the lender but can surprise borrowers if not reviewed in advance.

Encourage clients to ask: *"What's my exit timeline, and how does this loan support it?"*

Example:

A 5-year prepayment penalty on a 3-year value-add plan could cost the investor significant profit.

An agent aware of this can protect their client's financial flexibility by identifying such clauses early, discussing exit timelines with the lender, and ensuring the loan terms match the client's strategy before closing.

Debt Service Coverage Ratio (DSCR)

As discussed in Chapter 8 – Know Your Numbers, the DSCR reflects how comfortably a property's income covers its debt obligations.

When evaluating financing, remember that a DSCR above 1.25 generally signals stability and indicates that the property earns roughly 25 percent more than needed to pay the loan — a healthy margin.

Anything lower than that signals increased risk to lenders and should prompt a closer review of the deal's financial structure.

Example:

A property with $150,000 NOI and $120,000 in annual debt service = DSCR 1.25.

If NOI dropped to $110,000, the DSCR becomes 0.92 — a warning flag for both lender and agent.

How to Convey This to Your Client Confidently:

You might say —

"This number tells us how safely the property's income supports its debt.
At 1.25, there's enough cushion for the lender — the property makes about 25% more than needed to cover the loan.
If income dropped closer to 0.9, it means the property isn't earning enough to pay its debt comfortably, which could make refinancing or new financing more difficult.
So we want to aim for stability — where income comfortably supports the loan — not just barely meets it."

Delivering it this way keeps your explanation simple, factual, and supportive. **You're not giving lending advice** — you're interpreting what the number means in plain, confident language that empowers your client to make informed decisions.

In Practice — How the Core Metrics Connect

Think of NOI as the engine, Cap Rate as the market's lens, and DSCR as the lender's safety gauge. When all three align, the deal is both financeable and sustainable.

From Financing Knowledge to Advisory Authority

Financing mastery is about connecting numbers to decisions.

When you can explain how the type of loan, term length, and risk profile influence your client's strategy — without overstepping into lending advice — you become the voice of clarity and confidence in every transaction.

✍ **In Practice — Translating Financing into Strategy**

Choose one active or past multifamily deal and use it as a real-world learning lab.

Your goal is to understand how financing structure shapes the deal's story — and how to communicate that story with confidence.

Run two scenarios:

1. A fixed-rate loan with long-term stability.
2. A bridge loan with a 12-month repositioning goal.

Note the differences in cash flow, DSCR, and equity growth under each scenario — then explain them out loud as if you were teaching a client, student, or colleague.

💡 **Coaching Insight:**

Focus on clarity, not complexity. You don't have to sound like a lender — you just need to make the numbers make sense.

For example, if the bridge loan shows higher returns but greater short-term risk, practice phrasing it like this:

"This structure offers faster potential gains but comes with more moving parts. The fixed-rate option trades some of that upside for stability and predictability."

This exercise sharpens your ability to turn complex financial details into actionable, trustworthy guidance — the mark of a true multifamily professional.

Compare Actual vs. Pro Forma

Numbers tell a story — but not every story is true.

In multifamily real estate, two sets of financials often appear in a deal package: the actual income and expenses and the pro forma projections.

As previously discussed in Chapter 8 – Know Your Numbers, the pro forma represents projected or anticipated performance based on adjustments to rent, occupancy, or expenses — not current results.

An effective agent must know how to compare these figures, interpret the differences, and guide the client toward sound conclusions.

APPLIED APPLICATION — Reading Beyond the Spreadsheet

The actuals reflect how the property currently performs — the verified rent roll, collected income, and operating expenses as reported by the seller.

The pro forma, by contrast, represents what the property could generate after changes or improvements. It's a forecast, not a fact.

Example:
A property might show current rents averaging $1,150 per unit (actual), while the pro forma projects $1,275.
That's roughly a 10% increase — but until leases are renewed or units are improved, that upside remains theoretical.

Your role as an advisor is to help clients understand where the facts end and assumptions begin.

How to Communicate This to Your Client Confidently:

You might say —

"These numbers show us what the property is actually earning today versus what it could earn with certain improvements or rent increases. My goal is to make sure we base our decisions on what's real right now — while also understanding what's possible in the future."

Then, pause and guide the client through both sides of the analysis:

- Highlight the verified numbers (current rent roll, actual expenses).
- Contrast them with the projected numbers (expected rent growth, reduced expenses).
- **Ask,** *"What would have to happen for these projections to become reality?"*

That one question helps clients visualize the work, time, and risk between the actual and the pro forma.

➢ *Keynote:*
When agents frame the conversation this way, they shift from "selling a property" to consulting on a plan.

It builds trust, manages expectations, and demonstrates professional restraint — traits clients never forget.

Separating Assumption from Evidence

A clear-eyed real estate strategist looks at both sets of numbers and asks:

- Is the pro forma growth supported by market data?
- Are comparable properties achieving those projected rents?
- Do expenses seem reasonable, or have they been minimized to inflate the NOI?
- How much would a small difference in NOI impact value?

Example:

At a 6 percent capitalization rate, every $1,000 change in NOI equals roughly $16,600 in value.

That means a $5,000 NOI overstatement inflates the price by more than $83,000.

When you explain this to a client, it shifts the focus from speculation to precision.

You're no longer just reviewing numbers — you're protecting investment capital through factual interpretation.

Agents who can answer these questions demonstrate not only financial literacy, but integrity.

They bring transparency to the transaction and earn long-term trust from both investors and lenders.

To see how this plays out in practice, let's look at a real-world scenario that illustrates the difference between analysis and assumption.

💼 **In Practice Example — The Story Behind the Numbers**

Suppose a 20-unit building's pro forma claims a 5 percent expense ratio improvement compared to actuals.

You investigate further and discover that the seller reduced the "Repairs & Maintenance" line item by half and removed "Professional Management Fees" entirely from the pro forma.

That may look attractive on paper — but it's misleading in practice.

Your expertise allows you to say:

"If we reinstate realistic management and maintenance costs, this property's NOI decreases by $18,000 — which directly affects value and loan qualification."

By grounding the conversation in factual analysis, you protect your client from overpaying for projected performance that doesn't yet exist.

How to Communicate This with Confidence

You might say —

"The pro forma shows potential, but potential only matters if it's achievable. Let's look at what's happening right now — the current rents and expenses — and then determine whether the property's projections are realistic for this market.
My goal is to help you buy based on performance you can verify, not promises that may not materialize."

This approach builds credibility, encourages responsible decision-making, and distinguishes you as a data-driven professional — not a deal chaser.

Present Findings Professionally

Numbers only matter when they're communicated clearly.

After completing your analysis, your next responsibility is to present your findings in a professional, transparent format that helps the client make a confident decision.

Think of this step as the moment where credibility meets clarity.

APPLIED APPLICATION — Present with Precision

Once your financial review is complete, organize your findings into a concise, visual summary that tells the story behind the numbers — not just the numbers themselves.

Overview:

Start with the fundamentals — purchase price, NOI, cap rate, and cash flow. These create context for every discussion.

Highlights:

Identify the property's strengths and opportunities supported by tangible evidence, not assumptions.

Risks:

Provide a clear, honest assessment of potential concerns or limitations, explaining how each might affect financing, operations, or return

Transparency here builds credibility.

Conclusion:

End with your professional recommendation, framed through the client's goals and backed by measurable data.

Clients respect transparency; it builds trust, confidence, and long-term loyalty.

◆ **Agent-to-Investor Example Dialogue (data → decision)**

Agent: *"The property's NOI supports the asking price, but the pro forma assumes rent increases the market hasn't proven. My advice is to underwrite based on current performance, and treat the upside as potential."*

Investor: *"So we're not paying for hope — we benefit from it if it materializes?"*

Agent: *"Exactly. We buy the real performance, and we earn the upside if and when it's achieved."*

FIELD INSIGHT — The Hidden Gem

Erica, a multifamily agent, analyzed a small 10-unit building others had overlooked.

Her spreadsheet revealed rents were 20 percent below market and expenses inflated by outdated management.

She demonstrated to investors how modest upgrades could double cash flow within 18 months.

They purchased the property — and she gained three repeat clients from that one deal.

Her analysis didn't just sell a property; it built a reputation.

In multifamily real estate, analysis is the new marketing.

Reflection Questions

1. Do I verify data or rely on assumptions?
2. Which metrics do I still struggle to explain clearly to clients?
3. How can I strengthen the way I communicate numbers — visually and verbally?
4. What tools or templates can make my analysis process faster and more consistent?

Key Takeaways

- Numbers are tools, not tricks. Use them to inform, not impress.
- Transparency creates trust — and trust builds career longevity.
- Every accurate analysis is a silent marketing campaign for your professionalism.
- Your greatest value as an agent is your ability to translate complexity into clarity.

Every property tells a story — and every agent who learns to interpret that story gains more than just transactions; they gain professional mastery.

By now, you've learned that strategic deal analysis isn't about dazzling clients with data — it's about guiding them toward clarity. It's the art of combining verified numbers with real-world judgment, of balancing optimism with caution, and of building confidence through truth rather than persuasion.

Your role as a multifamily professional is not to predict the market, but to interpret it with integrity. When you help clients understand both opportunity and limitation, you become the voice of stability in a business defined by motion.

➢ ***Keynote:***

True analysis leadership means you can explain complex financial data in simple, actionable terms. When clients leave a meeting feeling both educated and empowered, you've done more than close a deal — you've built trust that multiplies.

Reflection Prompt

(Pause and consider before moving forward.)

- What's one area of deal analysis that now feels second nature to me?
- Where do I still hesitate — and why?
- How will I continue sharpening my analytical voice to serve my clients more powerfully?

🔳 LEADERSHIP CHALLENGE — From Analyst to Advisor

Choose one property or deal — whether real or hypothetical — and walk through every step from this chapter:

1. **Factor in Financing** — Compare loan structures and their impact on returns.
2. **Model Forced Appreciation** — Identify the levers that drive value.
3. **Compare Actual vs. Pro Forma** — Separate verified data from assumption.
4. **Present Findings Professionally** — Summarize your analysis with integrity.

Then, deliver a five-minute verbal presentation as if speaking to a client or investor.

Your goal: to turn your analysis into insight, and your insight into influence.

What's Next

In the next chapter, we extend analytical mastery beyond existing assets and into development and new construction — where value must be evaluated before income exists.

This expansion deepens your understanding of how multifamily opportunities are assessed across their full lifecycle, from stabilized performance to forward-looking feasibility.

What you've mastered in this chapter becomes the analytical language you will rely on as advisory decisions move beyond historical performance and into scenarios shaped by assumptions, timing, and disciplined judgment.

Chapter 10 — Multifamily Development & New Construction

Advanced Analysis When the Asset Does Not Yet Exist

Multifamily real estate sales are often introduced through existing income-producing properties — stabilized assets with operating histories, financial statements, and measurable performance. Yet a significant portion of multifamily opportunity exists before the first tenant ever moves in.

New construction, land acquisition, and development-adjacent transactions represent a different category of advisory responsibility — one that requires understanding, restraint, and strategic fluency.

This chapter is not about teaching agents how to become developers. It is about equipping professionals with development literacy — the ability to understand how multifamily development works, communicate intelligently with developers and investors, and advise ethically when the asset does not yet exist.

I. Existing Assets vs. Development Deals

Existing multifamily assets are evaluated through historical performance. Net operating income, expense ratios, rent rolls, and trailing financials form the foundation of valuation and risk assessment. Development deals, by contrast, are evaluated through assumptions.

In new construction and land-based transactions, value is not derived from what a property has produced, but from what it may produce in the future — if a sequence of events unfolds as planned.

This distinction is critical. Applying resale logic to development opportunities is one of the most common and costly mistakes agents make.

As discussed in Chapter 9, strategic deal analysis depends on reliable data.

In development scenarios, that data must be projected rather than observed — increasing the importance of judgment, discipline, and professional restraint.

Development valuation is forward-looking, conditional, and time-sensitive. There is no operating history to lean on, only projections that must be stress-tested against market demand, construction costs, regulatory approvals, and capital availability.

Advisors must understand this shift before attempting to guide clients through these conversations.

II. The Multifamily Development Lifecycle (Agent Perspective)

From an agent's standpoint, multifamily development follows a recognizable lifecycle, even though each project carries unique variables

It begins with land identification and site selection, followed by zoning analysis, entitlement approvals, and feasibility evaluation. Pre-development includes underwriting assumptions, capital planning, and architectural design. Construction transforms plans into physical assets, while lease-up and stabilization determine whether projections translate into performance.

Agents add value by recognizing where a project sits within this lifecycle and adjusting expectations accordingly. The role is interpretive, not operational. Understanding timing, dependencies, and risk exposure allows advisors to communicate responsibly — and to know when specialized expertise must be introduced.

III. Land & Site Acquisition for Multifamily

Land transactions differ fundamentally from income-property sales. Pricing is not anchored to NOI, but to potential. Raw land, entitled land, and improved sites each carry different risk profiles and pricing logic.

Assemblage — combining multiple parcels to create development-ready sites — adds further complexity. Highest and best use analysis becomes central, and misjudging zoning constraints or entitlement timelines can derail an otherwise attractive opportunity.

A parcel that appears attractively priced may carry hidden entitlement delays, density limitations, or infrastructure costs that materially change feasibility once examined beyond surface pricing.

For agents, the advisory responsibility lies in clarity. Land is valued for what it can become, not for what it currently produces. Communicating this distinction protects both the client and the professional.

IV. The Developer Mindset vs. the Investor Mindset

Developers and investors often use the same vocabulary, but they approach risk differently. Investors typically prioritize income stability, downside protection, and predictable returns. Developers assume extended timelines, upfront capital exposure, and uncertainty long before income materializes.

This mindset shift matters. Development conversations emphasize feasibility, sequencing, and contingency planning rather than immediate yield. Advisors who recognize this distinction avoid misaligned expectations and build credibility with sophisticated clients.

V. Valuation Without NOI

When NOI does not exist, valuation relies on feasibility models, cost-per-door analysis, replacement cost considerations, and absorption assumptions.

Pro Formas estimate future performance, but every projection depends on variables that can change.

For example: an existing 100-unit multifamily property may be valued using trailing NOI and a market-derived capitalization rate.

A proposed 100-unit development, by contrast, is evaluated using projected rental assumptions, estimated construction and stabilization timelines, cost-per-door metrics, and an assumed exit environment — all of which must perform as modeled for value to materialize.

Lease-up speed, rental demand, construction pricing, and exit assumptions all influence outcomes. Small deviations can materially affect value.

Advisors should understand these concepts well enough to explain them — and disciplined enough to avoid presenting projections as guarantees.

VI. Financing & Capital Stacks (High-Level Only)

Development capital structures are layered. Equity, debt, preferred returns, and the timing of capital deployment matter as much as interest rates. Construction loans differ from permanent financing, and the transition between them introduces both opportunity and risk.

Agents are not lenders or capital architects, but they must understand the basic structure well enough to recognize complexity and direct clients to appropriate professionals.

Knowing what not to explain is as important as knowing what to reference.

VII. Risk, Timing & Advisory Responsibility

Development risk is cumulative. Regulatory delays, cost overruns, market shifts, and financing constraints compound over time. Advisors must communicate uncertainty honestly and avoid overstating upside.

As explored in Chapter 8, leverage amplifies both opportunity and exposure.

In new development scenarios, that amplification occurs before income exists — increasing the importance of timing, structure, and disciplined advisory language.

Ethical practice requires clarity, documentation, and professional restraint.

When the asset does not yet exist, credibility becomes the agent's most valuable currency.

VIII. Where This Ends — And the Developer Path Begins

Development literacy elevates advisory capacity without crossing professional boundaries. This chapter is designed to introduce the concepts, language, and judgment required to engage thoughtfully with multifamily development and new construction — not to teach execution or advanced development strategy.

Agents who wish to pursue development more deeply must acquire additional education, capital experience, and operational exposure.

Those paths deserve dedicated study. Here, the goal is fluency: enough understanding to ask the right questions, recognize complexity early, and communicate responsibly in development-adjacent conversations.

Reflection Prompt

(Pause and consider before moving forward.)

As you consider multifamily development and new construction, reflect on where professional fluency ends and responsibility begins.

How does your advisory role change when the asset does not yet exist and value is based on assumptions rather than performance?

Consider how development literacy can strengthen your credibility without tempting you to overextend.

How will you communicate uncertainty, risk, and possibility in a way that maintains ethical boundaries, protects client trust, and reinforces your role as a disciplined advisor rather than a predictor of outcomes?

▩ LEADERSHIP CHALLENGE — Lead With Restraint When Certainty Is Absent

Identify a scenario in your market where a client, investor, or colleague is enthusiastic about a multifamily development or land opportunity but lacks complete information.

Your challenge is not to advance the deal — it is to elevate the conversation.

Practice slowing the discussion by clearly distinguishing between what is known, what is assumed, and what remains uncertain. Recommend appropriate next steps, including when to involve specialized professionals, rather than offering predictions or assurances.

Leadership in development-adjacent transactions is demonstrated not by confidence alone, but by the discipline to protect credibility when outcomes cannot yet be proven.

✍ Practice Exercise — Interpret Without Overstepping

Identify one multifamily development or land opportunity in your market.

Practice explaining:

What exists today

What could exist in the future

What assumptions must hold true

Do so without offering guarantees, projections, or promises.

Interpreting Risk Without Predicting Outcomes

New Development literacy does not make you a builder.

It makes you a strategic interpreter — able to translate vision, risk, and opportunity into responsible guidance.

What's Next

With development literacy in place, the analytical phase of this book is complete.

You now understand how multifamily assets are evaluated across their full lifecycle — from existing income-producing properties to opportunities where value must be assessed before income exists.

The chapters that follow move beyond formation and feasibility into long-term structure.

In the next chapter, the focus shifts to wealth strategies — how assets are positioned, protected, and guided over time so that financial insight becomes durable, intentional growth

PART IV

WEALTH, LEGACY & LEADERSHIP

Wealth is not created by isolated decisions — it is built through structured thinking over time.

In this part, you shift from analyzing individual deals to understanding the long-term structures that shape wealth outcomes over time.

Rather than concentrating on transactions in isolation, Part IV develops the fluency required to interpret how financing, taxation, leverage, and time interact — and to communicate those dynamics responsibly to clients making consequential decisions.

Here, you strengthen your ability to advise across cycles. You learn how capital structures influence resilience, how strategic choices compound over time, and how misalignment between strategy and structure can quietly erode value.

This perspective allows you to manage expectations, protect credibility, and guide conversations beyond short-term outcomes toward durability, flexibility, and long-term opportunity.

Part IV develops an ***ownership perspective*** — the lens required to interpret structure, risk, and consequence without assuming operational control.

Through this lens, analysis becomes strategy, and strategy becomes long-term direction — not through control, but through clarity.

Chapter 11 — Wealth Strategies and 1031 Exchanges

Wealth is not what you earn — it's what you keep and grow.

In multifamily real estate, wealth is created through what you keep, what you control, and how efficiently your capital moves.

This chapter takes you beyond transactions and into the structural mechanics of long-term wealth. It teaches you how equity grows, how investors preserve capital through the IRS 1031 Exchange, and how to architect the kind of financial legacy that outlives your client.

This is not just about investing.
This is about transforming income into freedom.

I. Understanding Wealth as Strategic Freedom

Money buys options. Wealth buys time.

True financial independence begins when investors stop relying on earned income and start engineering asset-based income that compounds without their daily effort.

This distinction separates financial motion from financial mastery:

- **Income earner:** trades time for money.
- **Wealth builder:** uses money to buy more time.

The goal — for you and your clients — is to operate entirely in that second identity, where cash flow stabilizes, equity expands, leverage works in your favor, and time becomes your greatest asset.

"You don't build wealth by saving more; you build it by owning more."

II. Equity Growth and the Mechanics of Appreciation

Equity is the difference between what a property is worth and what is owed on it.

But how equity grows is what separates amateur investors from sophisticated ones.

Multifamily equity grows through three primary mechanisms:

1. Market Appreciation

Organic value increases driven by:

- Rental demand
- Market expansion
- Development and Infrastructure growth
- Cap rate compression

2. Loan Amortization (Principal Paydown)

Each mortgage payment reduces debt — forced savings built into ownership.

3. Forced Equity (Value Creation)

Strategic improvements such as:

- Renovations
- Operational efficiencies
- Expense reductions
- Rent optimization
- Improved tenant quality

Forced equity is the investor's superpower.
It allows value to rise independent of the market.

➢ ***Keynote:***

Equity is unrealized wealth until you use it — through sale, refinance, or exchange.

III. The 1031 Exchange — IRS Rules, Timelines, and Investor Advantage

The IRS 1031 Exchange (Section 1031 of the Internal Revenue Code) is one of the most powerful wealth-preservation tools in U.S. tax law.

It allows investors to defer capital-gains taxes when selling one investment property and purchasing another of equal or greater value.

IRS Core Requirements

- **Investment Intent** — Both properties must be held for investment/business.
- **Equal or Greater Value Rule** — Reinvest equal or greater value to defer all taxes.
- **45-Day Identification Window** — Identify replacement properties in writing.
- **180-Day Purchase Window** — Close on an identified asset within 180 days.
- **Qualified Intermediary (QI)** — Investor cannot touch the funds.

Why Investors Use the 1031 Exchange

- Preserve net proceeds
- Increase buying power
- Scale portfolios faster
- Defer capital gains and depreciation recapture
- Compound equity across cycles

A 1031 Exchange is not tax elimination — it is tax deferral.

APPLIED EXAMPLE — Taxable Sale vs. 1031 Exchange

Scenario:

An investor sells a multifamily property for $500,000 with an adjusted tax basis of $200,000.

For illustration purposes only, the estimated capital gains and depreciation recapture taxes total approximately $75,000.

Option A — Taxable Sale

The investor completes a standard sale and pays the estimated taxes at closing.

- Gross sale proceeds: $500,000
- Estimated taxes paid: $75,000

Net reinvestable capital: $425,000

The investor now enters the next acquisition cycle with reduced purchasing power, limiting leverage capacity and deal size.

Option B — 1031 Exchange

Instead of triggering immediate tax liability, the investor utilizes a tax-deferred exchange structure.

- Gross sale proceeds reinvested: $500,000
- Taxes deferred, not eliminated

This preserves the entire equity position, allowing the investor to deploy more capital into the next acquisition.

Impact Over Time

The preserved $75,000 compounding across multiple acquisitions can grow into hundreds of thousands — even millions — over long horizons.

(For illustration purposes only. Advisors should encourage clients to consult tax and legal professionals for transaction-specific guidance.)

IV. The Power of Compound Exchanges

Each time an investor executes a 1031 Exchange, they preserve more capital for reinvestment.

One exchange preserves capital.
Multiple exchanges multiply capital.

But the real advantage isn't just tax deferral — it's momentum.

The Compounding Effect

When an investor defers taxes over multiple cycles, five forces begin compounding simultaneously:

- **Equity Preservation**
  Every dollar retained is a dollar that continues working.
  Over time, preserved capital becomes a silent partner fueling scale.
- **Full-Proceeds Reinvestment**
  Instead of reinvesting what *remains* after taxes, investors reinvest *everything* — accelerating the climb into larger, more stable assets.
- **Portfolio Upsizing**
  Each exchange typically moves the investor into higher-unit-count properties with stronger income, better management economies, and improved lending options.
- **Cash Flow Expansion**
  As unit count rises, income rises — often faster than expenses.
  This widens the investor's margin of safety and long-term stability.
- **Depreciation Reset Strategies**
  Not tax advice — conceptually, larger assets often carry larger depreciation schedules.
  (Advisors can highlight the concept — investors must consult a tax professional for specifics.)
- **Inflation Hedging**
  Larger assets typically outperform inflation due to rising rents, rising values, and rising replacement costs.

Why it Matters:

Your role is to help clients *see the runway,* not just the transaction in front of them.

When clients understand how exchanges compound, their investment horizon expands — and your advisory relationship deepens

A single exchange is helpful.
A sequence of exchanges becomes life-changing.

It allows an investor to leapfrog the years they would have otherwise spent trying to save their way into larger assets.

Example: A 20-Year Exchange Path

1. 4-unit → 8-unit
2. 8-unit → 16-unit
3. 16-unit→ 24-unit
4. 24-unit → 50-unit

Across each cycle:

- Taxes deferred
- Equity preserved
- Cash flow strengthened
- Stability increased
- Reinvestment power multiplied

This is how small investors become large portfolio owners.
Not through luck — through discipline, structure, and time.

> *Capital Compounds with Time and Intent*
> Advisors who understand this compounding effect can help clients plan decades ahead, not just one transaction at a time.
> This is where you shift from being an agent to a long-term strategist.

V. Mindset Shift — Think Like an Asset Manager, Not an Agent

An agent focuses on the next commission.
An asset manager focuses on the next decade.

Advisors who adopt asset-manager thinking deliver clearer guidance, earn deeper trust, and anchor decisions in long-term strategy.

What Asset Manager Thinking Looks Like

Asset managers think in terms of:

- Cycles, not closings
- Cash flow durability, not commission checks
- Equity trajectories, not price tags
- Long-term utility, not short-term wins

They evaluate every property through the lens of:

- Will this asset perform for 5–10 years?
- How will it behave in different market environments?
- What is the timeline for repositioning, refinancing, or exchanging?
- How does this property support the larger portfolio strategy?

Four Pillars of Asset Manager Mentality

1. Refinance Schedules
   Understanding when to unlock equity without disrupting cash flow.
2. Tax Strategy Awareness
   Recognizing how depreciation, cost segregation, and exchanges shape long-term outcomes.
   (Not tax advice — conceptual awareness.)
3. Estate & Continuity Alignment
   Seeing each asset as part of a long-term and intergenerational framework.
4. Reinvestment Timelines
   Thinking several moves ahead — not one transaction at a time.

Why it Matters:

When you adopt the long-term posture of an asset manager:

- your advice becomes richer
- your clients trust your depth
- your portfolio builds intentionally
- your financial outcomes expand through strategy
- you evolve from salesperson to steward — from agent to advisor

Your clients — and your future self — benefit when you adopt a long-term wealth posture.

VI. Leverage Refinancing Wisely

Refinancing is one of the most strategic tools in a real estate investor's wealth-building arsenal. When executed with clarity, discipline, and long-term intent, it allows investors to access equity without creating a **taxable event** — a unique advantage of real estate and a powerful lever for scaling portfolios.

But like any tool, a refinance only strengthens a portfolio when the timing, structure, and purpose are aligned.

Advisors guide this decision by helping clients understand not only what they can borrow, but what they *should* borrow based on performance, risk tolerance, and long-range objectives.

When Refinancing Strengthens a Portfolio

Refinancing adds value when three conditions converge:

- **Equity has meaningfully increased**
  Through appreciation, amortization, or forced value creation.
  This ensures the investor is unlocking performance — not speculation.
- **The new loan terms enhance stability**
  Lower interest, extended amortization, stronger DSCR, or improved cash flow spread.
  Better terms = better resilience.

- **The extracted capital has a productive purpose**
  Renovations, repositioning, or a new acquisition that grows future income. Refinancing is most powerful when it fuels progress — not consumption.

A refinance should expand the investor's margin of safety, not narrow it.

When Refinancing Becomes Risky

Refinancing is detrimental when it elevates risk instead of reducing it:

- **Cash flow tightens under the new loan**
  If monthly cushion shrinks, the refinance erodes stability rather than strengthening it.
- **Borrowing is used to patch operational shortfalls**
  This turns a temporary issue into a structural one.
- **Debt outpaces income growth**
  When leverage grows faster than performance, flexibility vanishes.

Over-leveraging doesn't just strain a portfolio — it reduces future opportunity.

The Advisor's Guiding Principle

Refinancing can release equity tax-free and reposition a portfolio for long-term success —
but only when executed from a place of strategy, not urgency.

Your guiding mantra:
Borrow against appreciation — not against optimism.

Advisors protect clients by ensuring:

- Cash flow remains healthy after the new loan
- Vacancy and expense stress-tests are passed
- Not all available equity is removed
- Refinancing supports long-term growth, not short-term relief
- Stability is never sacrificed for liquidity

This is how advisors help clients scale responsibly and avoid the trap of debt-driven fragility.

APPLIED EXAMPLE — CAPITAL PRESERVATION IN PRACTICE

A property valued at **$1,000,000** increases to **$1,300,000** through strategic improvements.

A refinance can pull capital for a new acquisition while maintaining DSCR and cash flow strength.

However —

If the increase was due only to a temporary, emotion-driven market, an aggressive refinance may overexpose the investor when conditions normalize.

Refinance performance — not hope.

Why it Matters:

Your role is to elevate the investor's perspective beyond the loan offer and into long-term portfolio health.

Advisors help clients ask:

- Does this refinance strengthen or weaken the portfolio?
- What happens to cash flow under the new terms?
- Will extracted capital create new income — or new strain?
- Is this a step toward scaling, or a step toward stress?

When refinancing aligns with long-term vision, it becomes a catalyst for exponential growth —
advancing not just the next deal, but the investor's entire wealth trajectory.

VII. Strategic Diversification Within Multifamily Portfolios

Diversification is not about owning different assets — it is about owning assets that behave differently under pressure.

Sophisticated investors diversify *within* the same asset class to reduce volatility, stabilize cash flow, and expand long-term opportunity.

The goal is not complexity —
the goal is resilience.

Why it Matters:

It balances risk, smooths income, and strengthens long-term resilience.

Advisors help clients diversify not by guessing, but by identifying complementary assets.

› Diversification Across Property Types

Examples include:

- small multifamily + a short-term or vacation rental
- local ownership + passive syndication
- stabilized assets + value-add assets

Each asset type responds differently to interest rates, tenant turnover, and economic cycles.

When blended intentionally, the overall portfolio becomes more stable than any single property.

› Diversification Across Markets

Balanced portfolios often combine:

- **appreciation markets** — long-term value growth
- **cash-flow markets** — stronger income today

This approach helps smooth performance when one market outperforms or underperforms the other.

› Diversification Across Strategy Layers

Sophisticated investors pair complementary strategies:

- **Core assets** — stability, lower risk
- **Value-Add assets** — higher potential, moderate risk
- **Opportunistic plays** — targeted, data-driven growth

Each layer contributes to a different part of the investor's financial objectives.

› How Advisors Guide Clients Through Diversification

Advisors help clients evaluate:

- risk tolerance
- liquidity needs
- investment horizon
- market familiarity
- tax posture
- legacy objectives

Diversification is not random — it is the structured alignment of assets to investor identity.

➤ Advisor Caution — Avoid Over-Diversification

Too much diversification:

- dilutes focus
- increases management strain
- complicates reporting
- reduces clarity around performance

A well-designed portfolio is diversified, not scattered.

➢ ***Keynote:***

Diversification safeguards your client's current portfolio while shaping the trajectory of their long-term growth.

APPLIED EXAMPLE — THE ADVISOR-LED DIVERSIFICATION CONVERSATION

Client: *"I want higher cash flow, but I also want long-term value. Should I pick one market or one strategy?"*

Advisor: *"Instead of choosing one, we design a blend.*
For example, we place a stabilized duplex in a strong-cash-flow market to give you predictable monthly income. Then we pair it with a value-add eight-unit in an appreciation market to grow long-term equity.
Both assets move differently, which protects you during interest-rate shifts, tenant cycles, and market fluctuations."

Client: *"So the goal isn't owning more — it's owning wisely?"*

Advisor: *"Exactly. Strategic diversification means your portfolio performs whether the market is calm or changing. It grows in two directions: cash flow today and equity tomorrow."*

VIII. Exit Strategy, Estate Planning, and Intergenerational Wealth

A true wealth plan does not end with acquisition — it ends with continuity.

Sophisticated investors design portfolios that outlive their decision-making years, and advisors play a critical role in helping them think through that horizon.

Your role is not to provide legal or tax advice —
your role is to provide clarity, structure, and strategic awareness so clients know which licensed professionals to bring to the table and when.

The Advisor's Four Pillars of Exit & Legacy Planning

1. **Timing Clarity**
   Help clients identify *when* assets are likely to be sold, exchanged, refinanced, or held long-term.

2. **Portfolio Role Definition**
   Not all assets serve the same purpose.
   Some are wealth accelerators, others are cash-flow anchors, and some become legacy holdings.

3. **Transfer Readiness**
   Advisors highlight the importance of organizing documentation, stabilizing operations, and simplifying structures before assets transfer to heirs.

4. **Continuity Planning**
   Clients must consider:
   • Who will manage the portfolio?
   • Who understands the systems you helped them build?
   • What values and decision frameworks should guide the next generation?

These conversations elevate you from "agent" to strategic wealth advisor in multifamily real estate sales.

In Practice — Preparing Clients for Legacy Planning

Use these prompts to help clients clarify their long-term plans:

- When will they sell?
- Which assets belong in exchange cycles — and which should be held long-term?
- Which properties should be refinanced rather than sold?
- How will heirs inherit assets?
- Should properties be held in trusts, LLCs, or partnerships?
- What protections are in place against liability or mismanagement?
- Who will manage the portfolio when the owner no longer can?
- What systems and documentation must be organized before transition?

This is not legal advice — it is conceptual clarity that positions you as a strategic advisor — while execution is handled by estate attorneys, CPAs, and planners.

APPLIED EXAMPLE — Guiding an Exit Strategy Conversation

Client: *"I'm not sure what to do with my properties when I'm ready to slow down. Should I just sell everything?"*

Advisor: *"Before deciding that, let's identify the purpose of each asset. Some may be ideal for exchanging into better-performing properties, while others might be perfect long-term holds for your heirs.*
From there, we can outline which professionals — like your CPA or estate attorney — should be involved to structure everything properly."

Client: *"I hadn't thought about each property having a different role."*

Advisor: *"Exactly. A strong legacy plan starts with clarity — not urgency. We build the roadmap now so transitions feel intentional, not reactive."*

▸ ***Keynote:***
Strategic advisory work happens in two dimensions:
how conversations are framed, and how capital decisions unfold over time.

FIELD INSIGHT — The Power of Deferred Taxes

Gloria purchased a four-unit building early in her career.
Fifteen years later, it doubled in value.

Instead of selling and paying six-figure taxes, she exchanged into a 12-unit asset.

- Her cash flow tripled.
- Her taxes deferred.
- Her portfolio expanded.

She didn't earn her way to wealth —
she exchanged her way there.

Reflection Questions

(Pause and consider before moving forward.)

- Do I treat commissions as income or investment seed capital?
- How many of my clients could benefit from understanding exchanges?
- What steps can I take this year to build my own portfolio?
- How will I teach my family what I am learning about wealth?

Key Takeaways

- Wealth is built through ownership, leverage, and reinvestment.
- 1031 Exchanges preserve capital and accelerate long-term growth.
- Refinancing and diversification create strategic mobility.
- Legacy is built through systems, wisdom, and intentional planning.

What's Next

You've learned how wealth is built in multifamily real estate — through ownership, equity growth, smart leverage, tax deferral, and disciplined reinvestment.

In the next part of this book, we move from wealth understanding to advisory execution — translating these principles into practical strategies for both your clients and your own portfolio.

You'll learn how to:

- integrate wealth strategy into client conversations
- design clear, long-term investment roadmaps
- position yourself as a trusted, forward-thinking professional advisor

You now understand how wealth works.

Next, you'll learn how to operate like a professional who helps build it — with intention, wisdom, and long-term responsibility.

Chapter 12 — Building A Legacy Through Real Estate, Wealth and Wisdom

Legacy is the final evolution of mastery.

It is what remains after the transactions are closed, the contracts expire, and the commission checks are long deposited.

It is the imprint of your leadership on the people you serve, the systems you create, and the wisdom you pass forward.

Multifamily real estate gives you the tools to build wealth.

Legacy teaches you how to use that wealth with intention, alignment, and impact.

This chapter expands your vision from strategic professional to architect of generational transformation. Because wealth is not the end — it is the beginning of what you can build for others.

I. Legacy as the Highest Form of Wealth

Legacy is not money — it is meaning.
In real estate, true legacy evolves in three dimensions:

1. **Financial Legacy** — the assets, equity, and cash flow you steward
2. **Intellectual Legacy** — the systems, skills, and strategies you document
3. **Human Legacy** — the people you lift, mentor, and empower

Assets can be inherited. But wisdom must be taught.
And impact must be lived.

This is why legacy is the highest form of wealth: it is the only wealth that continues compounding long after you are gone.

Your name is the first asset your family will inherit.
Protect it with excellence.

II. The Architecture of Legacy Wealth

Your legacy begins with the portfolio you build — but it expands through the discipline with which you manage, maintain, and transfer it.

A legacy-driven investor focuses on:

- Cash flow stability (DSCR, reserves, risk tolerance)
- Equity expansion (forced appreciation, rent growth, loan amortization)
- Tax efficiency (1031 cycles, depreciation, cost segregation)
- Strategic reinvestment (refinancing, repositioning, scaling)
- Long-term portfolio structure (LLC alignment, asset protection, succession clarity)

This is where Chapters 7–10 come full circle:
the negotiation mastery, financial literacy, deal analysis, and wealth strategies you've learned become the foundation of a portfolio that supports you… and outlives you.

Legacy wealth is not built through a single deal — it is engineered through disciplined cycles of intelligent ownership.

III. Educating the Next Generation — Teaching Wealth, Not Just Leaving It

Long-term real estate advisors understand that generational wealth often fails because the next generation is handed assets without being handed understanding of how it's generated and maintained.

As a legacy-aware professional, your role is not to instruct heirs — but to recognize when education, planning, and the right advisory team are essential.

Families who succeed across generations understand:

- What cash flow is and Why it Matters
- How mortgages, equity, and leverage work
- How to interpret a rent roll
- The purpose of reserves
- How appreciation actually occurs
- Why long-term ownership creates stability
- How to make decisions based on data, not emotion

Make wealth a conversation, not a secret.
Make money a tool, not a taboo.

"Wealth is rarely lost to misfortune — it is lost to misunderstanding."

When your families understand the language of real estate, they inherit not just property — they inherit power.

IV. Systems — The Silent Heirloom

Buildings can be sold.
Money can be spent.
But systems outlive everything.

Your systems — the way you run your business, analyze deals, communicate, negotiate, and lead — are the blueprint future generations can use to sustain, grow, and preserve your legacy.

Document:

- Deal analysis templates
- Your acquisition criteria
- Negotiation scripts
- Your CRM structure
- Renewal and retention workflows
- Due diligence checklists
- Your investment philosophy
- Your leadership values

This is your intellectual infrastructure.
Systems are the bridge between your success and someone else's start.

V. Succession Planning for a Multifamily Professional

Legacy requires foresight.

Whether you own properties, run a team, or operate a personal brand, think through:

- Who will run the assets?
- What processes will continue without you?
- How will your business transition?
- What roles will your heirs play?
- What guidance will they need?
- What values must be preserved?

This is not legal advice — it is conceptual clarity.

You are not simply building a portfolio.
You are building a continuity plan for the vision, discipline, and excellence you've practiced across your career.

VI. Impact as the Ultimate Return on Investment

Legacy extends beyond financial gain.

Impact amplifies wealth into meaning:

- Mentor emerging agents
- Provide education to your community
- Donate to housing initiatives
- Invest in local revitalization
- Sponsor real estate scholarships
- Teach what no one taught you

Income creates comfort.
Impact creates legacy.

Your greatness is not measured by how much you acquire —
but by how many people rise because you existed.

VII. The Legacy Letter — Your Final Gift of Guidance

Take time to write a Legacy Letter — a document for future generations that captures:

- what you learned
- what you value
- what you believe
- how you overcame obstacles
- what you hope your family continues
- how you want your assets to support their purpose

A Legacy Letter is not about instructions.

It is about inspiration.

It is the emotional cornerstone of everything you've built.

FIELD INSIGHT — The Compounding Effect of Legacy

Angela purchased her first four-unit building early in her career.

Instead of selling for a quick profit, she exchanged it.

Then exchanged again.

Then again.

Over 20 years:

4 units → 8 units → 16 units → 24 units → 50 units

Through disciplined ownership, tax-efficient strategy, and the intentional education of her children, she built a portfolio that not only created wealth — it created direction for the next generation.

Her family didn't inherit "*property.*"

They inherited wisdom, stability, and opportunity.

Angela didn't earn her way into legacy —
she engineered it through intention.

Reflection Questions

(Pause and consider before moving forward.)

- What do I want my life to stand for?
- What systems am I passing forward?
- Who am I teaching, mentoring, or preparing?
- How will my real estate portfolio support others after me?
- What do I want the next generation to understand about wealth?

Key Takeaways

- Legacy is the highest expression of wealth.
- Wealth must be taught, not just transferred.
- Systems and wisdom outlast assets.
- Impact turns success into significance.
- You build legacy every day through how you lead, teach, and serve.

Advisors who think clearly lead confidently.

Your reasoning becomes your competitive advantage.

What's Next

You've now reached the philosophical summit of Part IV — where strategy meets identity and where your role transcends transactions.

In the next section, you'll transition from internal mastery to outward influence: how to lead, teach, speak, and position yourself as a multifamily authority in your market and beyond.

You'll move from the mechanics of wealth to the mechanics of leadership, and from portfolio growth to professional impact that multiplies your reach and reputation.

Your legacy begins now — in the choices you make, the people you empower, and the wisdom you pass forward.

Chapter 13 — Advisor Performance Scorecard

Success in multifamily real estate requires more than motivation, ambition, or even experience. It requires measurability — the ability to evaluate your performance with honesty, clarity, and discipline.

Top advisors don't wait for the market, a manager, or a client to tell them where they stand. They score themselves, track their growth, refine their weaknesses, and reinforce their strengths long before anyone else notices a shift.

This chapter gives you the same tools elite professionals use to stay ahead of the curve.

Your performance is no longer vague or emotional — it becomes structured, specific, and actionable.

When you understand the metrics behind your effectiveness, you can change the trajectory of your career with intention rather than chance.

I. Understanding Advisor Performance at a Professional Level

Great advisors are not defined by their busiest months — they are defined by their repeatable systems.

Performance is predictable when:

- expectations are clear
- behaviors are consistent
- metrics are evaluated regularly
- adjustments are strategic, not reactive

High performers in every field — sales, investment banking, asset management, consulting — share one truth:
They measure what matters, and they measure it consistently.

In multifamily advisory work, this means tracking:

- Productivity
- Lad generation
- Follow-up consistency
- Communication quality
- Deal flow health
- Market knowledge
- Financial literacy
- Negotiation readiness
- Client experience

These elements form the foundation of your performance scorecard.

II. The Advisor Performance Scorecard

Your performance scorecard is divided into three categories:

Category 1: Skill Competency

How well you execute the core responsibilities of a multifamily advisor.

Score yourself on a scale of 1–5:

1 — Needs Development
2 — Inconsistent
3 — Competent
4 — Strong
5 — Expert-Level Mastery

Skills to Score:

- Market knowledge
- Deal analysis
- Client communication
- Prospecting systems

- Negotiation setup
- Financial conversation fluency
- Presentation strength
- Lead nurturing
- Time management discipline

Category 2: Production Indicators

What your numbers reveal about your consistency and discipline.

Evaluate quarterly:

- Total new leads generated
- Number of meaningful conversations
- Number of qualified investors/prospects added
- Number of property tours completed
- Number of proposals/presentations delivered
- Number of offers prepared
- Number of deals closed

Numbers don't lie — they tell you what your habits produce.

Category 3: Leadership Behaviors

The mindset and habits that determine long-term success.

These are qualitative — but critical:

- Do you communicate proactively?
- Do you prepare before every call/meeting?
- Do you maintain emotional discipline?
- Do you follow through on commitments?
- Do you solve problems or wait for direction?
- Do you bring clarity or confusion to clients?
- Do people feel confident after interacting with you?

Score: Developing → Emerging → Consistent → Strong → Exemplary

III. Quarterly Assessment Framework

Every quarter, evaluate:

1. **What did you plan?** (List your goals.)
2. **What did you execute?** (List your real actions.)
3. **What worked?** (Identify wins, patterns, and areas of strength.)
4. **What didn't?** (Identify gaps, missed steps, inconsistent behaviors.)
5. **What must change?** (Precise, actionable adjustments — not vague desires.)

Quarterly consistency creates annual excellence.

IV. Confidence & Competency Test

Confidence without competence creates errors.
Competence without confidence limits opportunity.
You need both.

Confidence Test — Rate 1–5

- I can explain multifamily fundamentals clearly.
- I can present a deal with authority.
- I can guide investors through financial concepts.
- I can communicate uncertainty without losing credibility.
- I can lead a client through hesitation or doubt.

Competency Test — Rate 1–5

- I understand valuation mechanics (cap rates, NOI, sensitivity).
- I can diagnose a deal's weaknesses quickly.
- I can interpret rent rolls without confusion.
- I can prepare investors for financing structures accurately.
- I can negotiate without rushing, reacting, or retreating.

Your lowest scores tell you exactly where to focus next.

V. Advisor Performance Grid (Quarterly Score)

Create four columns:

Q1 | Q2 | Q3 | Q4

For each quarter, assign:

- Performance Score (1–5)
- Production Score (1–5)
- Leadership Score (1–5)

Then calculate:

Quarterly Advisor Index (QAI)

(Average of all three categories)

This number — more than feelings, hopes, or effort — reveals your professional trajectory.

APPLIED EXAMPLE — QUARTERLY ADVISOR INDEX (QAI)

Scenario:

You've completed your Q1 self-evaluation.

Category	Score (1-5)	Notes
Performance Score	3	Solid financial and market understanding, but inconsistent deal analysis workflow.
Production Score	2	Low meaningful conversations and inconsistent follow-up during February.
Leadership Score	4	Strong communication, timely client updates, effective problem-solving.

Step 1 — Calculate QAI:

(Performance + Production + Leadership) ÷ 3

→ (3 + 2 + 4) ÷ 3 = 3.0 QAI

Step 2 — Interpret the Score:

A QAI of 3.0 indicates a competent but inconsistent quarter.

This score suggests:

- You have strong leadership instincts.
- You possess solid skill fundamentals.
- Your production habits are the bottleneck, not your knowledge or communication ability.

Step 3 — Set the Next Quarter Priority:

Focus Area for Q2 = Production (Score: 2)

Examples:

- Commit to 3 meaningful conversations per day.
- Build a 5-day follow-up cadence.
- Run one weekly deal review for consistency.

QAI is a compass, not a judgment.

It shows exactly where to apply effort so your growth becomes measurable, strategic, and controlled.

APPLIED APPLICATION — The Professional Reset Cycle

Use this when:

- your pipeline feels slow
- your confidence dips
- you lose momentum
- deals fall through
- clients go cold
- communication feels messy

The Reset Cycle:

1. Score yourself honestly
2. Identify the lowest category
3. Focus on one skill for 7 days
4. Re-score
5. Adjust one behavior
6. Move to the next metric

This is how professionals rebuild momentum with intention.

> 💼 **In Practice — "Clarity Removes Anxiety"**
>
> Most advisor fear doesn't come from lack of talent...
>
> It comes from not knowing where they stand.
>
> When you track your performance, you reduce fear.
>
> When you measure your growth, you build confidence.
>
> When you hold yourself accountable, you become unstoppable.

The Difference Between Busy and Effective

Busy advisors talk to everyone.

Effective advisors track who matters.

Busy advisors rely on memory.

Effective advisors rely on systems.

Busy advisors hope for momentum.

Effective advisors build it deliberately.

This scorecard makes that difference visible.

▩ LEADERSHIP CHALLENGE — THE 30-DAY ACCOUNTABILITY SPRINT

For the next 30 days:

- Score yourself daily
- Track one metric consistently
- Identify one skill to elevate
- Eliminate one distracting behavior
- Add one leadership habit

At the end of 30 days, your performance identity will not be the same.

Reflection Questions

(Pause and consider before moving forward.)

1. What performance category reveals your biggest opportunity for growth?
2. What behavior must change for your next level?
3. What skill would immediately improve your results if strengthened?
4. What metric will you begin tracking daily?

What's Next

In the next chapter, you'll shift from testing what you know to preparing to demonstrate it — aligning your skills, judgment, and leadership with the standards expected in certification-level and professional evaluations.

PART V

LEGACY, LEADERSHIP & LONG-TERM INFLUENCE

True success is measured not only by what you build — but by what endures.

In this final part, you step beyond accumulation and into stewardship.

The focus expands from portfolio performance to purpose, continuity, and influence.

Here, wealth is no longer viewed as an endpoint, but as a responsibility — something to be structured, protected, and transferred with intention.

Part V challenges you to think at the level of legacy. You'll explore how investors prepare for transitions, how advisors guide clients through succession and estate considerations, and how disciplined strategy creates opportunity not just for one generation, but for those that follow.

This is where professional expertise intersects with leadership, ethics, and long-range vision.

These chapters are designed to help you integrate everything you've learned — mindset, analysis, strategy, and communication — into a coherent philosophy of practice. One that supports not only transactions, but trust; not only growth, but continuity.

This is where mastery becomes leadership — and leadership becomes lasting impact.

Chapter 14 — Mastery Review Section

At this stage in your journey, you have gained the frameworks, language, and analytical tools of a multifamily professional.

But true mastery is not whether you understand the concepts — it is whether you can apply them consistently across real-world scenarios with clarity, confidence, and strategic judgment.

Mastery is revealed not in theory, but in pressure.
Not in familiarity, but in decision-making.
Not in what you know, but in how you think.

This chapter is designed to challenge your judgment, stretch your reasoning, and calibrate the way you analyze problems. Every advisor reaches a point where knowledge must convert to wisdom — and this is where that evolution occurs.

The questions, scenarios, and application problems ahead will strengthen your strategic thinking and prepare you for the level of leadership required in complex multifamily transactions.

I. The Purpose of Mastery Review

Mastery Review is not a test — it is a mirror.

Its purpose is not to rank you, certify you, or expose shortcomings for correction by others. It exists to help you see yourself clearly — as a professional responsible for judgment, leadership, and trust.

In multifamily advisory work, outcomes are shaped long before decisions are finalized. Mastery Review examines the quality of your thinking, not just the correctness of your conclusions. It reveals how you engage with complexity when answers are incomplete and stakes are real.

Through this review, you gain visibility into:

- How you process information
- How quickly you identify risk
- How accurately you interpret opportunity
- How well you articulate your analysis
- How consistently you apply your frameworks

II. Chapter-by-Chapter Mastery Questions

Each set of mastery questions is designed to test the depth of your understanding, not just your memory.

From Chapter 7 — Negotiation Mastery

- What is the strategic purpose of silence in negotiation?
- How does pace influence negotiation power?
- What are the indicators that a client's non-negotiables are unclear?
- How do perception and positioning shape client confidence?

From Chapter 8 — Financial Literacy

- Explain cap rate compression in your own words.
- What does a rent roll reveal about operational stability?
- When analyzing leverage, what ratio matters most for safety — and why?
- Why does forecasting separate advisors from agents?

From Chapter 9 — Deal Analysis

- What is the "*first glance*" filter and why does it matter?
- How do you determine whether a deal deserves deeper modeling?
- Explain sensitivity analysis in plain terms.
- When presenting findings, what creates professional credibility?

From Chapter 10 — Wealth Strategies

- What is the fundamental purpose of a 1031 exchange?
- How does forced equity create long-term wealth independence?
- Why is loan amortization considered “built-in savings”?

From Chapter 11 — Legacy & Leadership

- How does legacy differ from achievement?
- What systems must outlive you to create true legacy?
- Why is letting go a form of leadership?

III. Case Study Scenarios

These scenarios require analytical reasoning — not memorization.

› Case Study 1: The Unstable Rent Roll

A 32-unit property shows:

- 4 recent move-outs
- 6 leases expiring within 60 days
- 2 units on notice
- Delinquency at 12%

Question:

What three risks would you highlight for your investor, and what would you recommend as next steps?

› Case Study 2: The Overpriced Listing

The seller markets a property as an “8% cap.”

Your analysis reveals it is actually a 6% cap based on real NOI.

Question:

What is the advisor's role, and how should you communicate this discrepancy?

› Case Study 3: The Investor Hesitation

Your buyer is approved, interested, and in a strong financial position — but suddenly becomes paralyzed by indecision.

Question:

What leadership behaviors should you demonstrate to move the deal forward ethically and confidently?

IV. Real-World Application Problems

These sharpen your computational and diagnostic thinking.

› Problem 1: NOI Shift

NOI increases by $22,000 annually.
Cap rate = 6%.

Question:

What is the change in property value?
(Show reasoning steps when answering.)

› Problem 2: Leverage Risk Check

Purchase price: $1,500,000
Loan amount: $1,125,000

- What is the LTV?
- What does this tell you about leverage safety?

› Problem 3: Sensitivity Check

If expenses rise 5% annually but rent growth stays flat:

- What happens to cash flow?
- What does this signal to an investor?

› Problem 4: Price Your Offer

Seller wants $4.2M.
Your analysis supports $3.85M.

Exercise:

Draft the advisor-level justification you would present alongside your offer, clearly explaining how pricing, performance, and risk alignment support your position.

APPLIED APPLICATION — Advisor Mastery Review Rubric

Use this rubric to evaluate your completion and accuracy.

Rate each domain from 1–5:

- Clarity of explanation
- Accuracy of interpretation
- Correct use of financial concepts
- Ability to identify risk
- Communication strength
- Strategic recommendation quality

This rubric can be used in formal certification evaluations — mastery requires a minimum average of 4+.

💼 In Practice — "Your Thinking IS Your Value"

Clients don't hire you for your access.

They hire you for your interpretation.

Investors don't follow your steps.

They follow your judgment.

Mastery Review strengthens the part of you that clients trust most: ***the way you think.***

➢ *Keynote:*

Two advisors can receive the exact same information —
and produce completely different conclusions.

The advisor who wins is the one who:

- ◆ sees clearly
- ◆ interprets accurately
- ◆ communicates simply
- ◆ recommends confidently

This chapter develops those muscles.

▩ LEADERSHIP CHALLENGE — The Mastery Audit

For the next seven days:

Choose one case study or problem per day

- Complete it without notes
- Explain your reasoning out loud
- Identify where your logic felt uncertain
- Track patterns in your thinking

Mastery is built through repetition and reasoning — not by accident.

Reflection Questions

(Pause and consider before moving forward.)

1. Which section challenged you the most?
2. What skill gap became most visible?
3. Which scenario revealed your blind spot?
4. What is the next step in strengthening your professional judgment?

Key Takeaways

- Mastery is the ability to apply knowledge with precision.
- Judgment improves through structured scenarios and analysis.
- Advisors who think clearly lead confidently.
- Your reasoning becomes your competitive advantage.

What's Next

In the next chapter, you'll shift from testing what you know to preparing to demonstrate it — aligning your skills, judgment, and leadership with the standards expected in professional and certification-level evaluations.

Chapter 15 — Certification Preparation & Professional Readiness

Certification is not a badge — it is evidence.

Evidence of competence.

Evidence of discipline.

Evidence of mastery.

In multifamily real estate, credibility is built through the precision of your knowledge, the strength of your judgment, and the consistency of your execution.

A certification — whether internal, brokerage-based, or industry-recognized — signals to clients and peers that you hold yourself to a measurable professional standard.
This chapter prepares you for that standard.

Certification readiness is less about memorizing facts and more about demonstrating the thinking, skills, and behaviors expected of high-level advisors.

Your ability to synthesize information, interpret variables, and deliver clarity under pressure is what creates trust — and trust is the currency of leadership.

The tools, questions, and checklists in this chapter will sharpen your ability to work with accuracy, confidence, and professional excellence.

I. Understanding Certification Readiness

Certification exams test more than knowledge. They test:

- your ability to think critically
- your ability to interpret financial data
- your ability to diagnose risk
- your ability to communicate with authority
- your ability to lead clients through uncertainty

Readiness comes from:

- understanding concepts
- applying them consistently
- demonstrating them under pressure

Your goal is not simply to pass a test —
your goal is to embody excellence.

II. Instructor Notes — The Advisor Preparation Framework

These notes represent the internal guidance typically given by instructors or senior advisors during professional certification.

1. Master the Foundations Before the Formulas
An advisor should never memorize a formula they do not conceptually understand.

Clarity precedes calculation.

2. Accuracy Matters More Than Speed
Your first job is to be right.
Your second job is to be fast.

Speed grows from accuracy, not the other way around.

3. Explain Concepts in Plain English
If you cannot explain a concept clearly, you do not truly understand it.

Clients trust clarity.

4. Know What to Look For Before You Look at the Numbers
Certification requires pattern recognition:

What matters? What is noise? Where is risk? Where is opportunity?

5. Demonstrate Professional Judgment
Certification is not about being perfect — it's about thinking like a leader.

III. Competency Checklist — Certification-Level Skills

Use this checklist to evaluate your readiness.

Rate yourself: Not Yet • Emerging • Competent • Strong • Mastery

› Conceptual Competencies

- Understand cap rates, NOI, and cash flow mechanics
- Interpret rent rolls, T-12s, and pro formas
- Explain leverage risk and financing structures
- Identify operational red flags
- Evaluate deals using first-layer and second-layer analysis

› Communication Competencies

- Present deals clearly and persuasively
- Communicate financial concepts in plain language
- Manage investor hesitation with confidence
- Deliver professional recommendations
- Prepare advisory-level proposals

› Analytical Competencies

- Conduct sensitivity analysis
- Evaluate upside potential
- Compare debt structures
- Calculate valuation shifts
- Identify and quantify risk

› Leadership Competencies

- Guide clients through uncertainty
- Demonstrate emotional discipline
- Maintain a structured follow-up system
- Lead conversations instead of reacting to them
- Bring clarity and confidence to every interaction

A certification-ready advisor scores Strong or Mastery in at least 80% of these categories.

IV. Professional Knowledge Assessment — 50 Questions

This assessment represents a comprehensive evaluation of your conceptual, practical, financial, and advisory readiness.

Section A — Foundations & Mindset

1. What is the difference between motivation and purpose?
2. Why is identity important in advisory work?
3. What does "ownership thinking" mean?
4. How does long-term vision impact multifamily success?
5. Why is clarity more valuable than confidence?

Section B — Industry & Client Fundamentals

6. What defines an ideal multifamily client?
7. What is the purpose of a market intelligence system?
8. Why must an advisor understand financing structures?
9. What makes a prospect "qualified"?
10. What role does daily prospecting play in pipeline stability?

Section C — Communication Mastery

11. Why is tone translation important?
12. What does proactive communication accomplish?
13. How do you simplify complex information?
14. Why does empathy increase efficiency?
15. What is the purpose of a client retention system?

Section D — Negotiation Mastery

16. What is the strategic purpose of silence?
17. Why is pace important in negotiation?
18. What shapes client confidence during negotiation?
19. What creates a win-win negotiation outcome?
20. Why should non-negotiables be clarified early?

Section E — Financial Literacy

21. Define NOI.
22. What is cap rate compression?
23. Why is forecasting important?
24. What can a rent roll reveal?
25. What is the difference between pro forma and actuals?

Section F — Deal Analysis

26. What is the "first glance" filter?
27. Why conduct sensitivity analysis?
28. How does layered analysis work?
29. What creates persuadable evidence?
30. What does upside potential indicate?

Section G — Wealth Strategies

31. What is the purpose of a 1031 exchange?
32. Why does equity growth matter?
33. What is forced equity?
34. Why is loan amortization important?
35. What is strategic diversification?

Section H — Advisor Leadership

36. What is the advisor's primary leadership responsibility?
37. Why is emotional discipline essential?
38. What distinguishes an advisor from an agent?
39. What does influence look like in practice?
40. Why must systems outlive you to create legacy?

Section I — Applied Professional Judgment

41. Identify two risks in a delinquent rent roll.
42. What should you highlight in an overpriced listing?
43. How do you communicate uncertainty professionally?
44. What investor questions matter most when evaluating a deal?
45. What creates advisor credibility?

Section J — Advanced Mastery

46. How do rising expenses affect cash flow?
47. Why does leverage influence risk?
48. What is the purpose of a professional presentation?
49. Why does judgment matter more than memory?
50. What does a certification signal to the market about you?

▹ ***Keynote:***

Clients cannot see your internal discipline, they see your standards.

Certification reveals the professionalism you've built long before you earned the credential.

Certification Makes Excellence Visible

ADVISOR INSIGHT — THE ANATOMY OF READINESS

You are ready when:

- your judgment is consistent
- your analysis is accurate
- your communication is clear
- your confidence matches your competence
- your leadership is intentional

Readiness is not a feeling — it is a result.

▩ LEADERSHIP CHALLENGE — THE 14-DAY READINESS SPRINT

For the next 14 days:

1. Complete 10 knowledge questions per day.
2. Review 1 case study from Chapter 13.
3. Read 1 financial concept aloud.
4. Rewrite 1 explanation in simpler terms.
5. Practice 1 advisory conversation scenario.

In 14 days, your confidence will shift from emotional to evidence-based.

Reflection Questions

(Pause and consider before moving forward.)

1. Which competency requires the most development?
2. How prepared do you feel to demonstrate your knowledge under pressure?
3. What concept becomes clearer each time you explain it?
4. What behavior or habit will strengthen your readiness?

Key Takeaways

- Certification is proof of excellence.
- Readiness requires clarity, consistency, and practice.
- Competency is strengthened through evaluation.
- Professional judgment is your most valuable asset.

What's Next

In the next chapter, you'll translate readiness into rhythm — using practical planning tools and operating systems to sustain mastery in real time and across an entire career, not just a testing environment.

Chapter 16 — Professional Planning Tools

The Systems That Sustain Mastery

A high-performing advisor is not built by talent alone — they are built by structure.

Structure creates consistency.

Consistency creates results.

Results create momentum.

Momentum creates mastery.

Professional growth is rarely accidental. It is engineered through routines, planning systems, accountability structures, and clear performance alignment.

In multifamily real estate, you do not rise by doing more — you rise by doing what matters most, consistently and strategically.

This chapter gives you the essential planning tools used by top advisors to maintain clarity, drive measurable progress, and build a long-term performance identity.

These tools allow you to navigate seasons, stay grounded during volatility, and accelerate during opportunity.

I. The Architecture of Professional Growth

Sustained professional growth requires three foundations:

1. **Clarity** — Knowing what you are aiming for — not vaguely, but specifically.
2. **Consistency** — Executing on the behaviors that produce results — even when motivation fades.
3. **Accountability** — Tracking your actions, measuring your performance, and adjusting with intention.

The tools in this chapter are built around these three pillars.

When implemented with discipline, they transform the advisor experience from reactive to strategic.

II. Annual Growth Blueprint — The Macro Vision

Your annual plan establishes the direction of your year and the identity you are stepping into.

› Annual Vision Statement

Define:

- the advisor you are becoming
- the market-level impact you intend to make
- the professional standard you expect of yourself

Write it in the present tense:

"I am an advisor who…"

› Annual Metrics That Matter

Track only the metrics that drive meaningful change:

- Deals submitted
- Deals closed
- Investors added to database
- Total meaningful conversations
- Gross commission income
- Average deal size
- Advisor Index Score (A.I.S.)

› **Annual Growth Priorities (Top 3)**

Identify the three priorities that will create the greatest professional shift. Examples:

- Strengthen financial fluency
- Build a stronger investor pipeline
- Increase deal flow consistency
- Improve communication confidence
- Become negotiation-ready year-round

› **Annual Leadership Commitments**

Define the behaviors you will embody consistently:

- I communicate before clients ask.
- I prepare before every meeting.
- I follow up with discipline, not emotion.
- I protect my focus and energy.
- I build value before asking for opportunity.

III. Monthly Goals & Metrics Tracker

Monthly planning bridges your annual vision to your daily behaviors.

A. Monthly Goals (Top 5)

Choose five high-impact goals.

Each goal must be:

Clear. Measurable. Time-bound. Aligned.

Examples:

- Complete 20 meaningful conversations
- Add 15 qualified investors
- Conduct 5 property tours
- Analyze 3 new deals
- Publish 1 market snapshot

B. Monthly Performance Metrics

- Track the following:
- Total leads generated
- Conversations held
- Follow-up attempts
- Deals reviewed
- Offers prepared
- Deals submitted
- Deals closed

C. Monthly Reflection

At the end of each month, evaluate:

1. What worked?
2. What didn't work?
3. What will you adjust next month?

Clarity builds momentum.

IV. Weekly Execution Map — The Real Engine of Progress

Weekly execution determines your consistency.

This is where real transformation occurs.

A. Weekly Revenue-Producing Actions

➢ These matter more than anything else:

- Prospecting
- Follow-up
- Investor calls
- Deal reviews
- Property tours
- Offer preparation
- Negotiation preparation

B. Weekly Planning Blocks

➢ Every Monday:

- Review priorities
- Set targets
- Schedule calls
- Identify top prospects
- Assign follow-up tasks
- Plan marketing touches

➢ Every Friday:

- Review progress
- Score performance
- Identify next week's focus

C. Weekly Performance Score (1–5)

➢ Score yourself based on:

- Effort
- Consistency
- Focus
- Professionalism
- Follow-through

This weekly score becomes your most honest accountability partner.

V. Daily Advisor Alignment Sheet

Your day is your mirror.

Your habits reveal your trajectory.

A. Morning Alignment

➢ Answer these three questions:

1. What is the most important thing I must accomplish today?
2. What conversations matter most?
3. How will I bring clarity and leadership to my clients?

B. Midday Reset

➢ At midday:

- Reevaluate priorities
- Refocus your attention
- Remove distractions
- Regain strategic posture

C. End-of-Day Reflection

➢ Ask yourself:

1. What did I complete?
2. What did I avoid?
3. What will I carry into tomorrow?

Small daily alignments compound into massive professional growth.

APPLIED APPLICATION — The Advisor Operating System (AOS™)

This is a simplified, repeatable operating system for advisors. When these tools are integrated, they form a single operating rhythm.

Daily:

- Morning alignment
- 2 hours of prospecting
- 3 meaningful conversations
- 1 deal review
- 1 follow-up sequence

Weekly:

- Prospect list refresh
- Deal pipeline review
- Client updates
- Market snapshot review

Monthly:

- Performance analysis
- Goal alignment
- Professional development commitment

Quarterly:

- Full Advisor Performance Scorecard
- Leadership evaluation
- Strategic reset

This system creates advisors who dramatically reduce the risk of falling behind.

> Talent creates opportunity.
> Discipline converts opportunity into results.
> Professionals don't rely on inspiration —
> they rely on structure.

💼 **In Practice — The Power of Managerial Self-Leadership**

Before you can lead clients, you must lead yourself.

Your consistency becomes your credibility.
Your structure becomes your brand.
Your follow-through becomes your reputation.
A self-led advisor is never truly behind.

They are always building forward.

▩ LEADERSHIP CHALLENGE — The 21-Day Professional Reset

For the next 21 days:

1. Use the Daily Alignment Sheet.
2. Complete 1 hour of follow-up.
3. Complete 1 deal analysis.
4. Track your Weekly Performance Score.
5. Conduct a Weekly Review.
6. Hold yourself accountable to one leadership behavior.

At the end of 21 days, your professional identity will shift from reactive to strategic.

Reflection Questions

(Pause and consider before moving forward.)

1. Which planning tool will have the biggest impact on your consistency?
2. What behavior consistently disrupts your momentum?
3. How will you strengthen your professional structure this year?
4. What will you commit to doing daily to support your long-term vision?

This is where discipline becomes identity.

Key Takeaways

- Structure sustains mastery.
- Planning transforms potential into progress.
- Advisors grow when performance becomes intentional.
- Leadership begins with self-management.

What's Next

You have completed the core curriculum of Mastering Multifamily Real Estate Sales — from mindset and communication to financial literacy, deal analysis, wealth strategy, legacy, and professional systems.

From here:

- Use Appendix A–D as your extended toolkit.
- Lean on the Glossary + Acronyms as your reference.
- Consult the Index to revisit concepts as your deals become more complex.

This is no longer just a book.

It is now your operating manual, teaching framework, and professional playbook.

You are ready to step into the market not just as an agent, but as a multifamily advisor, strategist, and leader.

What you build next depends on what you practice starting now.

APPENDIX A

Commercial & Multifamily Real Estate Acronyms and Abbreviations

(Comprehensive Reference for Advisors, Investors, and Educators)

A

A.I.S. — Advisor Index Score

Performance scoring system evaluating advisory consistency and professional execution.

AM — Asset Management

Oversight of operations, financial performance, and property-level strategy.

AOM — Amount of Money

Common shorthand used in financial evaluation.

ARM — Adjustable-Rate Mortgage

Loan with an interest rate that adjusts at predetermined intervals.

ARV — After-Repair Value

Estimated value of a property after improvements.

AUM — Assets Under Management

Total capital or property assets actively managed by an advisor or firm.

B

BEP — Breakeven Point (Breakeven Occupancy)

Occupancy level required for revenues to cover operating expenses and debt service.

BOV — Broker Opinion of Value

Professional, non-appraisal valuation from a broker.

C

CAF — Common Area Fees

Charges related to the maintenance of shared spaces.

CAPEX — Capital Expenditures

Large, non-recurring expenses for improvements or replacements.

CF — Cash Flow

Net operational income remaining after expenses and debt service.

CMBS — Commercial Mortgage-Backed Securities

Loans pooled and sold as investment securities.

COC / CoC — Cash-on-Cash Return

Annual cash return relative to cash invested.

CRE — Commercial Real Estate

Income-producing property categories including multifamily, retail, and office.

CRM — Customer Relationship Management System

Platform for tracking client interactions, follow-ups, and communication cadence.

D

DD — Due Diligence

Verification period including inspections, financial review, and risk assessment.

DSCR — Debt Service Coverage Ratio

NOI divided by debt service; indicator of financing safety.

E

EGI — Effective Gross Income

Income after accounting for vacancy and loss-to-lease.

EMD — Earnest Money Deposit

Buyer deposit held in escrow showing transactional commitment.

F

FMR — Fair Market Rent

Government-published rental benchmarks.

G

GPR — Gross Potential Rent

Total rent possible if all units were leased at market rate.

GRM — Gross Rent Multiplier

Valuation shortcut comparing price to gross income.

I

IO — Interest-Only Period

Loan structure where only interest is paid for a set time.

IRR — Internal Rate of Return

Long-term, annualized return metric accounting for time value of money.

L

LLC — Limited Liability Company

Entity structure that provides liability protection for ownership.

LOI — Letter of Intent

Non-binding document outlining key deal terms before a contract.

LTC — Loan-to-Cost Ratio

Loan amount relative to total acquisition + improvement cost.

LTL — Loss to Lease

Difference between market rent and actual collected rent.

LTV — Loan-to-Value Ratio

Loan amount relative to property value; primary leverage measure.

M

MFR — Multifamily Real Estate

Residential properties with 5+ units.

MF — Multifamily

Short form for multifamily properties.

MLS — Multiple Listing Service

Property database system used by licensed agents.

M&O — Maintenance and Operations

Combined cost category for building upkeep.

N

NOI — Net Operating Income

Revenue minus operating expenses; primary valuation foundation.

NN / NNN — Double Net / Triple Net Lease

Lease structures where tenants cover varying levels of expenses.

O

OER — Operating Expense Ratio

Operating expenses divided by effective gross income.

OPEX — Operating Expenses

Operational costs required to run the property.

P

P&L — Profit and Loss Statement

Financial document summarizing revenues and expenses.

PGI — Potential Gross Income

Total income if all space is leased at contract rates.

PPU — Price Per Unit

Acquisition price divided by number of units.

PPSF — Price Per Square Foot

Acquisition price divided by total rentable square footage.

PM — Property Manager / Property Management

Operational oversight of tenant, maintenance, and rent collection.

PTI — Price-to-Income Ratio

Affordability metric comparing housing cost to local income.

R

R&M — Repairs and Maintenance

Recurring operational expenses for upkeep.

REIT — Real Estate Investment Trust

Structured trust investing in commercial assets; publicly or privately traded.

ROI — Return on Investment

Performance metric evaluating efficiency of capital investment.

RUBS — Ratio Utility Billing System

Utility cost-sharing method billing tenants proportionally.

T

T-12 — Trailing 12-Month Financials

Full-year operating statement.

T-3 — Trailing 3-Month Financials

Short-term, recent operations snapshot.

V

VAC — Vacancy Loss

Lost income due to unoccupied units.

VAR — Value at Risk

Advanced risk-analysis measurement.

APPENDIX B

WORKSHEETS, TEMPLATES & ANALYSIS TOOLS

(For Advisors, Students, Instructors, and Professional Application)

SECTION 1 — Advisor Performance & Planning Tools

1. Advisor Daily Alignment Worksheet

(Used by advisors to maintain clarity and focus)

Morning Alignment

1. The most important outcome I must achieve today is:
2. The conversations that matter most today are:
3. I will bring clarity and leadership today by:

Midday Reset

1. What must be refocused or clarified?
2. What distractions must be removed?

End-of-Day Reflection

3. What did I complete?
4. What did I avoid?
5. What must carry into tomorrow?

2. Weekly Execution Map

(Core engine of advisor progress)

Weekly Revenue-Producing Priorities

- Prospecting
- Follow-up
- Investor conversations
- Deal reviews
- Property tours
- Offer packaging
- Negotiation preparation

Weekly Targets

- Conversations: ________
- Follow-up sequences: ________
- Deals analyzed: ________
- Offers prepared: ________
- Pipeline touches: ________

Weekly Review

1. What moved my pipeline forward?
2. What created resistance or delay?
3. What will I improve next week?

3. Monthly Goals & Metrics Tracker

Monthly Goals (Top 5)

1.
2.
3.
4.
5.

Monthly Metrics

- New investors added: ________
- Conversations held: ________
- Deals reviewed: ________
- Offers written: ________
- Listings evaluated: ________
- Tours completed: ________
- Deals submitted: ________
- Deals closed: ________

Monthly Reflection

1. What was my strongest habit this month?
2. What slowed me down?
3. What will I adjust next month?

SECTION 2 — Market Intelligence & Deal Screening Tools

4. First-Glance Deal Filter

(Determines whether a property deserves deeper review)

Minimum Standards Checklist

❒ Submarket stability

❒ Rent roll consistency

❒ Vacan❒cy within acceptable range

❒ Expense ratio within typical range

❒ Property condition aligned with asking price

❒ No immediate "deal killers"

Three Essential Questions

1. Does this property meet minimum return expectations?
2. Is the submarket stable or improving?
3. Does its physical condition justify the list price?

Preliminary Decision

❒ Proceed to deeper review

❒ Request clarification from listing agent

❒ Decline and move on

5. Rent Roll Diagnostic Sheet

Key Indicators to Examine:

- Total leased units: ________
- Vacant units: ________
- Units on notice: ________
- Concessions: ________
- Delinquencies: ________
- Lease expirations (next 60–90 days): ________

Advisor Interpretation Notes:

6. T-12 Diagnostic Checklist

Verify the Following:

❐ Revenue consistency

❐ Expense discipline

❐ Repairs & maintenance abnormalities

❐ Utility cost trends

❐ Insurance or tax spikes

❐ NOI stability

Advisor Notes:

7. Cap Rate & Valuation Worksheet

Inputs

NOI: $__________________

Market Cap Rate: ________ %

Calculation

Value = NOI ÷ Cap Rate

Advisor Notes / Interpretation:

---

8. Sensitivity Scenario Worksheet

Variable Selected

❒ Income change

❒ Expense change

❒ Vacancy change

❒ Cap rate shift

Describe the scenario:

Outcome Impact

- Value change: ___________________________________
- Cash flow change: _________________________________
- Risk interpretation: ________________________________

9. Offer Justification Template

(Used to craft advisory-level offer explanations)

Property Address: ___________________________________

Seller's Asking Price: _________________________________

Advisor Supported Price:__________________________________

Evidence Summary

- Expense verification: ________________________________
- Rent roll alignment: _________________________________
- Market comps: ______________________________________
- Condition adjustments: ________________________________
- Income/expense stabilizations: __________________________

Advisor Statement

"Based on verified financials, market conditions, and operational data, the supported valuation for this asset is $________. This offer reflects accurate performance, realistic forecasting, and a fair opportunity for both parties."

SECTION 4 — Client & Communication Tools

10. Investor Discovery Call Sheet

Client Goals

☐ Cash flow

☐ Appreciation

☐ Tax strategy

☐ Diversification

☐ Long-term scaling

Discovery Questions

1. What is your ideal investment outcome?

2. How do you evaluate risk?

3. What is your preferred financing structure?

4. What is your timeline for your next acquisition?

5. What concerns typically slow your decisions?

Advisor Notes:

11. Prospecting Conversation Framework

Open with Value

"Here's a quick submarket update that may impact your portfolio…"

Discovery Question

"I'd love to understand how you're positioning your investments for next year — what matters most to you?"

Resource Offer

"I can send you a rent trend report or an updated comp set — which would you prefer?"

Next Step

"Let's revisit this on ________. I'll have updated data ready."

---

12. Communication Cadence Plan

Weekly Communication Target

- Investor follow-ups: ________
- Market updates sent: ________
- New connections made: ________
- Pipeline touches: ________

Monthly Communication Targets

- Newsletter or insight share
- Market summary
- Personal outreach to top clients

APPENDIX C

CASE STUDIES & INSTRUCTOR NOTES

(For Advanced Application, Classroom Use & Professional Development)

SECTION 1 — Instructor Guidance & Usage Notes

These case studies are designed for:

- classroom discussion
- advisor training
- certification evaluation
- professional workshops
- self-paced judgment testing

They focus on ***reasoning*** rather than memorization and reflect the complexity of real multifamily scenarios without stepping into lending or legal instruction.

How to Use These Case Studies

Instructors and readers should emphasize:

- **Interpretation** — *"What does this data tell us?"*
- **Risk Identification** — *"Where are the weak points?"*
- **Opportunity Recognition** — *"What could be improved or stabilized?"*
- **Communication** — *"How would I explain this clearly to a client?"*
- **Professional Recommendation** — *"What action makes sense next?"*

These are the same skills evaluated in professional–level mastery assessments.

SECTION 2 — Case Study Scenarios (With Instructor Notes)

Case Study 1 — The Unstable Rent Roll

› Scenario

A 32-unit property shows:

- 4 recent move-outs
- 6 leases expiring within 60 days
- 2 units on notice
- Delinquency at 12%

Instructor Notes — What This Tests

- Understanding of operational stability
- Ability to evaluate risk quickly
- Communication clarity under uncertainty

Questions for the Advisor

1. What three risks should be highlighted?
2. What next steps would you recommend to the investor?

Expected Advisor-Level Thinking

- Highlight turnover risk, income instability, and renewal uncertainty
- Recommend clarifying: lease-renewal probabilities, upcoming maintenance, rent-ready timelines, tenant quality patterns, and delinquency resolution
- Suggest next steps: request T-3 rent roll, delinquency report, updated leasing activity, and management commentary

Instructor emphasis:
Reasoning, not formulas.

Case Study 2 — The Overpriced Listing

› Scenario

The seller markets a property as an "8% cap,"
but verified financials show a **6% cap** based on actual NOI.

Instructor Notes — What This Tests

- Ability to avoid taking marketing language at face value
- Professional communication tone
- Ethical advisor guidance

Questions for the Advisor

1. What is your role in this situation?
2. How would you communicate the discrepancy professionally?

Expected Advisor-Level Thinking

- Clarify supported value through evidence
- Present findings factually, not confrontationally
- Provide a range supported by actual performance
- Explain how assumptions differ from real operations

Instructor emphasis:

Professional tone and data-driven communication.

Case Study 3 — The Hesitant Investor

› Scenario

Your investor is:

- approved
- liquid
- interested
- in a stable financial position
  …but suddenly becomes indecisive.

Instructor Notes — What This Tests

- Leadership presence
- Emotional discipline
- Communication clarity
- Decision-support skills

Questions for the Advisor

1. Which leadership behaviors matter most here?
2. How do you guide without pushing?

Expected Advisor-Level Thinking

- Recenter the conversation around goals
- Provide clarity, not pressure
- Address hesitation using logic and reassurance
- Reinforce decision criteria already agreed upon
- Keep the investor grounded in facts and long-term strategy

Instructor emphasis:
Confidence without coercion.

SECTION 3 — Application Problems (Analytical + Judgment)

Problem 1 — NOI Shift

› Scenario

NOI increases by $22,000 annually.
Market cap rate: 6%

◆ **Task**

What is the change in value?

Instructor Notes — What This Tests

- Basic valuation literacy
- Ability to interpret impact, not just compute it

Expected Advisor Reasoning

Value change ≈ NOI ÷ cap rate
$22,000 ÷ 0.06 = $366,667 increase in value

Instructor emphasis:
Understanding what the increase means for negotiations, offer ranges, or repositioning strategy.

Problem 2 — Leverage Safety Check

› Scenario

Purchase price: $1,500,000
Loan amount: $1,125,000

◆ **Task**

1. What is the LTV?
2. What does that imply about leverage safety?

Instructor Notes — What This Tests

- Risk literacy
- Ability to interpret leverage, not teach lending

Expected Advisor Reasoning

LTV ≈ 75%
Interpretation: Reasonable leverage, but still sensitive to income shifts.

Instructor emphasis:
Risk awareness — not lending guidance.

Problem 3 — Sensitivity Check

› Scenario

Expenses rise 5% annually; rent growth stays flat.

◆ **Task**

What happens to cash flow, and what does that signal?

Expected Advisor Thinking

- Cash flow compression
- Pressure on NOI
- Higher operational risk
- Need to evaluate expense drivers

Instructor emphasis:
Understanding volatility.

Problem 4 — Offer Support Logic

› Scenario

Seller's asking: $4.2M
Advisor-supported value: $3.85M

◆ Task

Craft a professional justification.

Instructor Notes — What This Tests

- Communication precision
- Ability to justify conclusions with clarity
- Professional tone in valuation conversations

SECTION 4 — Instructor Evaluation Rubrics

These rubrics are designed for:

Certification programs

- Brokerage training
- Continuing education workshops
- Self-assessment

1. Scenario Judgment Rubric

Rate (1–5):

- Clarity of Explanation
- Accuracy of Interpretation
- Identification of Risk
- Strength of Recommendation
- Communication Tone
- Professional Logic Flow

Mastery score = 4+ average

2. Communication Performance Rubric

Rate (1–5):

- Tone clarity
- Message structure
- Ability to simplify concepts
- Client-facing professionalism
- Emotional discipline
- Confidence without pressure

3. Analysis & Reasoning Rubric

Rate (1–5):

- Reasoning steps
- Evidence use
- Practical interpretation
- Economic awareness
- Decision alignment with client goals

APPENDIX D

ADDITIONAL PROFESSIONAL RESOURCES

(Tools, references, and systems to support mastery in multifamily advisory work.)

SECTION 1 — Market Intelligence & Data Sources

These resources help advisors stay informed, interpret trends, and strengthen investor-facing conversations.

Primary Market Data Platforms

- **CoStar** — Commercial property data, comps, leasing trends
- **REIS / Moody's Analytics** — Market vacancy, rent growth, absorption forecasts
- **Yardi Matrix** — Multifamily rent comp data, construction pipelines
- **RealPage** — Operational and rent-performance analytics
- **Zumper & Apartment List** — Rent trends for Class B/C submarkets

Local/Regional Data Sources

- **County tax assessor databases** — Property records
- **Local economic development authorities** — Job growth initiatives
- **MLS systems (GAMLS, FMLS, etc.)** — Verified sales, smallermultifamily deals
- **State housing authority reports** — Affordability trends, demographic shifts

SECTION 2 — Professional Organizations

Useful for continuing education, networking, and credibility building.

- **NAR (National Association of REALTORS®)**
- **NMHC (National Multifamily Housing Council)**
- **CCIM Institute** — Investment/financial training
- **IREM (Institute of Real Estate Management)**
- **ULI (Urban Land Institute)** — Development insights
- **Local Chamber of Commerce / Business Clubs**

SECTION 3 — Advisor Tools & Systems

These tools support productivity, client engagement, and organizational clarity.

Client & Pipeline Management

- CRM systems (e.g., Follow Up Boss, HubSpot, RealtyBackOffice), selected based on advisor scale, workflow complexity, and client engagement needs
- Lead-tracking spreadsheets
- Prospecting cadence templates

Deal & Property Analysis Tools

(Structured for interpretation, not lending guidance)

- Rent-roll review checklist
- T-12 high-level variance checklist
- Market snapshot templates
- Submarket scoring worksheet

Communication Tools

- Advisory call scripts
- Email follow-up templates
- Owner-outreach scripts
- Investor education one-pagers

Planning & Accountability

- Monthly metrics sheet
- Weekly execution map
- Daily alignment sheet
- Quarterly Advisor Performance Scorecard (from Chapter 13)

SECTION 4 — Professional Development & Skills Building

Optional resources for continuing growth, depending on the agent or brokerage.

Books (Advisor/Leadership Focused)

- *The Slight Edge* — Jeff Olson
- *Deep Work* — Cal Newport
- *Atomic Habits* — James Clear
- *The Psychology of Money* — Morgan Housel
- *Never Split the Difference* — Chris Voss

Skill-Focused Learning

- Negotiation workshops
- Communication skill seminars
- Financial-literacy modules
- Presentation & public-speaking training

Instructor note:
These materials supplement mastery — they do not replace the frameworks in this book.

SECTION 5 — Templates Included in This Book (For Quick Reference)

- Daily Advisor Alignment Sheet
- Weekly Execution Map
- Monthly Goals & Metrics Tracker
- Annual Growth Blueprint
- Advisor Performance Scorecard
- Mastery Review Rubric
- Instructor-Ready Case Study Set
- Certification Preparation Framework
- Professional Planning Tools (Chapter 16)

GLOSSARY

This glossary provides clear, practical definitions of the key terms, metrics, and concepts used throughout Mastering Multifamily Real Estate Sales.

The language in this book is intentional. Many terms carry technical meaning, strategic implication, or industry-specific nuance. This section exists to ensure consistency, precision, and shared understanding — allowing you to communicate with confidence, interpret opportunities accurately, and apply concepts correctly in real-world advisory situations.

When clarity matters, return here.

A

Absorption rate — market demand indicator; lease-up expectations; *see also* **Market intelligence**

Active listening — communication mastery; client clarity; *see also* **Tone translation**, **Empathy**

Advisor Index Score (A.I.S.) — performance scoring; quarterly evaluation; *see also* **Performance systems**

Advisor identity — professional evolution; mindset shift; *see also* **Mindset**, **Leadership**

Appreciation

market appreciation — value trends

forced appreciation — value creation; operational strategy; *see also* **Equity growth**

Asset management thinking — long-term ownership mindset; portfolio strategy

B

Broker Opinion of Value (BOV) — valuation overview; market comparison

Building systems — operational function; maintenance considerations; *see also* **Due diligence**

INDEX

This index is designed to help you quickly locate key concepts, frameworks, tools, and strategies throughout the book.
Use it as a reference when preparing for client conversations, reviewing material, or revisiting specific topics as your practice evolves.

D

E

F

G

I

L

M

N

P

Q

R

S

T

U

V

W

Z

FULL LEGAL & PROFESSIONAL PRACTICES DISCLAIMER

This book is for **educational and informational purposes only**. Nothing in this publication constitutes, or should be interpreted as:

- legal advice
- tax advice
- lending or mortgage underwriting guidance
- investment, financial, or fiduciary advice
- accounting, compliance, or regulatory guidance
- guarantees of results, income, financing approval, or investment returns

Real estate laws, lending guidelines, underwriting standards, tax regulations, and financial markets change frequently and vary by state and jurisdiction. Readers must consult with licensed professionals before making decisions involving:

- financing, loans, interest rates, mortgage structures
- tax planning, 1031 exchanges, capital gains strategies
- contracts, entity formation, asset protection, legal matters
- investment purchases, deal structuring, risk assessment, valuation
- underwriting, credit qualification, or lending decisions
- Return metrics in this book are presented for instructional illustration and assume stable equity conditions unless otherwise stated.

NO PROFESSIONAL RELATIONSHIP CREATED

Reading this book does not create any agent–client, advisor–client, legal, financial, or fiduciary relationship between the reader and the author, publisher, or contributors.

ACCURACY NOT GUARANTEED

Although every effort has been made to ensure accuracy, the author and publisher make no representations or warranties regarding completeness, timeliness, applicability, or accuracy of the information presented.
All information is provided "as is."

USE AT YOUR OWN RISK

Readers assume full responsibility for any decisions made based on the concepts, strategies, examples, or illustrations in this book. Neither the author nor the publisher shall be liable for any damages or losses arising from reliance on this material.

NO ENDORSEMENT OF THIRD PARTIES

Any references to lenders, financial institutions, platforms, tools, frameworks, or service providers are for illustrative or educational purposes only and do **not** constitute endorsements or recommendations.

FAIR HOUSING COMPLIANCE STATEMENT

The author adheres to all federal, state, and local Fair Housing laws.

Any references to tenants, occupancy, or markets are for educational illustration only and do not endorse discriminatory practices.

Advertising & Solicitation Disclaimer

This book is not an advertisement for investment properties or financial products.

Examples do not constitute offers or solicitations.

Results & Earnings Disclaimer

No financial guarantees or outcome promises are made or implied.

Real estate performance varies based on execution, conditions, and individual circumstances.

Anti-Fraud & Anti-Misrepresentation Notice

Readers may not represent this content as legal, tax, or lending instruction.

Readers may not claim to be certified by the author unless an official program exists and is completed.

E&O & GOVERNING LAW REFERENCE

The following reference clarifies professional responsibility, classroom use, and governing law.

Errors & Omissions (E&O) Disassociation Clause

The author's personal E&O insurance does not extend to reader actions or brokerage activities.

Readers must follow their own brokerage rules, state laws, and compliance requirements.

Instructor & Classroom Use Notice

This book may be used in classrooms, brokerages, or training programs.

Instructors are responsible for ensuring state compliance and licensing boundaries.

Jurisdiction & Governing Law

Any disputes related to this book are governed by the laws of the State of Georgia.

SERVICE AND LEADERSHIP

No journey of mastery is ever taken alone.

To every student, agent, advisor, instructor, and industry leader who has trusted me, challenged me, or invited me into their professional growth — thank you.

Your questions, your ambition, and your commitment to excellence have shaped the vision and depth of this book.

To the multifamily community — the brokers, lenders, analysts, operators, and educators who enrich this industry every day — your work is the backbone of opportunity for millions. Your dedication continues to inspire a higher standard of service and leadership.

And to every reader stepping into this field with courage and intention:

You are the future of multifamily real estate.

May this book serve as your blueprint, your mentor, and your strategic advantage.

— LS. Shepherd

ABOUT THE AUTHOR

LS. Shepherd is a multifamily real estate advisor and the creator of the Mastering Multifamily Real Estate Sales system — a practical, structured approach that blends mindset mastery, communication strength, financial understanding, and deal analysis into a unified professional framework.

Her experience in residential and multifamily advisory work has given her insight into how agents grow, how investors make decisions, and how clarity and discipline shape long-term success. She specializes in breaking down complex concepts and turning them into tools working professionals can use immediately.

Through LSS Publishing & Media, LLC, she develops strategic resources and professional materials that help real estate advisors operate with confidence, accuracy, and purpose.

Her mission is simple: elevate the standards of the industry while empowering others to build sustainable success and long-term impact.

FINAL NOTE TO THE READER

You now hold a professional roadmap — one that can elevate your career, sharpen your thinking, and position you as a strategic advisor in one of the most transformative sectors of real estate.

Return to it often.

Teach from it.

Grow through it.

And lead others with the clarity and confidence you've gained.

Your mastery is just beginning.

www.ingramcontent.com/pod-product-compliance
Ingram Content Group UK Ltd.
Pitfield, Milton Keynes, MK11 3LW, UK
UKHW020214290926
15470UKWH00001B/176

9 798995 021506